THEY ARE NOT YET LOST

True Cases of Psychic Detecting

Finding Victims, Tracking Villains
and Bringing the Lost Home

Dan Baldwin

They Are Not Yet Lost

A Four Knights Press Publication

Printed in the United States of America

* * * * *

Disclaimer

They Are Not Yet Lost is a Four Knights Press publication and not a product of the Find Me organization or Arizona Search Track and Rescue.

* * * * *

Front cover design by Gary Cascio. LateNite Grafix, Inc.
Front cover photo © 2015 Gary Cascio.LateNite Grafix, In
Formatting by Debora Lewis arenapublishing.org

ISBN-13: 978-1519638496
ISBN-10: 1519638493

Acknowledgments

A special thanks to Gary Cascio and LateNite Grafix of Santa Fe who designed the front cover and who provided the photo that appears in it.

Debbie Lewis and Arena Publications for excellent formatting and back cover design.

Tom Tilton, Mediation of Tucson.

Sharon Lashinger, Society of Southwestern Authors.

Contents

Dedication

Kelly Townsend and Julia D'Alfonzo

"When love speaks, the voice of all the gods make heaven drowsy with the harmony."

Shakespeare

Preface by Dan Baldwin

From 2001 until 2015 I was a member of Find Me, a group of psychics, retired and active law enforcement personnel, and legal and forensic specialists dedicated to finding missing persons and solving crimes. I was an inaugural member of that organization and served as a board member and officer. I also served as a volunteer "ground pounder" with the group's sister organization, Arizona Search Track and Rescue. As a pendulum dowser, I have searched with my "rock on a string" and with my feet on the ground from Colorado to California and throughout the deserts and mountains of Arizona. My dowsing skills have been used worldwide.

This book relates some of the most interesting cases investigated by Find Me. In addition to my own working files, the Find Me organization made available to me its original case files and notes. I also interviewed key persons involved in the investigations. This is a remarkable story of a remarkable group of people. I hope you find the book as interesting as I found the work.

Dan Baldwin

"The man who, in a fit of melancholy, kills himself today may have wished to live had he waited a week."

~Voltaire

CHAPTER ONE: ED HATFIELD

Find Me investigations begin with an email, such as this one.

FROM: KELLY SNYDER

TO: FIND ME

SENT: Tuesday, May 09, 2006 10:34 a.m.

RESPONSE IS "IMMEDIATE" 24-48 HOURS

EDWARD H. HATFIELD

DOB: 11-09-1957

POB: Winston-Salem, NC TOB: 7:33 p.m.

Edward went missing on April 29th, 2006 at 2:15 p.m. which is the last time anyone has spoken to him. His vehicle was found on I-17 at mile marker #310 approximately 26 miles south of Flagstaff, AZ on April 30th, 2006.

We may be doing a canine search in the next day or two, so don't wait… send your information ASAP.

Kelly

Ed Hatfield took a final drag off his cigarette and watched the smoke filter through the limbs of the pine tree. Surely a thought about his dreams going "up in smoke" must have crossed his mind as he smoked another and then another. He checked the ties that bound him to the tree and stared across the rugged beauty of Rattlesnake Canyon.

The pine and spruce forest took on a shimmer of gold from a dying sun and the bottom of the canyon was already growing dark in shadow. Except for the stale odor of cigarette smoke, the air was fresh and clean. He had selected a beautiful location. He let the cigarette drop and it landed on the pine straw among the others. All was peaceful and even the traffic noise from I-17, out of sight and just down the hill, was nothing more than a quiet hum. A gentle breeze carried a hint at the cold night ahead, so Ed took swallow of whiskey and then another. Sometime later the bottle joined the small scattering of cigarettes at the base of the tree. Like the growing darkness below, his depression must have deepened.

Perhaps his thoughts turned briefly to North Carolina or to Rhonda or to the fruitless job search just down the road in Phoenix. He might have grinned sadly at the smoke fading to nothingness – fading like all his prospects for a happy future. No one will ever know. Ed grasped his.38 revolver and put a violent end to his depression.

FILED AND FORGOTTEN

The date was April 29, 2006 and Rhonda Younger was a worried woman. She and her fiancé, Ed Hatfield, were in the process of moving from North Carolina to Phoenix, Arizona. In fact, Ed had been in the state capital some six week looking for work in the construction industry. The housing bubble and the healthy business climate in Arizona meant a lot of good work for a lot of men and women in the field. But things hadn't worked out for Ed. He had still not found a job. His failure was frustrating. Everywhere he looked in The Valley of the Sun he saw an explosion of construction – houses, businesses, shopping centers, high rise buildings and business centers. And he couldn't find a single company to take him on.

Rhonda had stayed behind in the Tar Heel State to sell her home and take care of all the last minute details a cross-country move entails. Ed temporarily moved in with her daughter, Brenda, and Brenda's husband, Joel. Rhonda was excited about starting a new and better life in Arizona, a better life that was eluding Ed. Then the phone calls started.

Ed phoned his friends to say he was going away for a while. Ed's failure to find work had been depressing, but it was clear that his depression had slipped into something deeper, something darker. He left the house saying he was getting a hotel room until Rhonda arrived, which was the agreement he had made previously with Joel and Brenda.

Ed's last conversation with Rhonda was about 2:15 in the afternoon. His mood was darker than usual and the brief conversation sounded more like a final goodbye than anything else. She could tell from the background noise that he was outside. His breathing was labored and his sentences broken. She could tell he was walking, perhaps hiking up hill.

That same day Officer Byrd of the Arizona Department of Public Safety located Ed's 2002 burgundy Dodge Ram truck at mile marker #310 on I-17 south of Flagstaff. The keys were still in the vehicle and the owner was nowhere in sight. The truck appeared to have been abandoned. There was no indication of foul play so Officer Byrd filed an abandoned vehicle report and had the truck impounded under report #2006023585. The vehicle was quickly delivered to the Automotive Services Camp Verde, AZ impound lot. Officially, Ed Hatfield was not yet a missing person. The police are reluctant to automatically classify a missing adult as a missing person. From their point of view, the opinion is understandable. From the point of view of friends and family, the view is unforgivable.

A cursory search of the area immediately surrounding the vehicle was conducted by the Yavapai Forest Patrol on April 30. Neither Ed nor any evidence of his presence in the area was discovered. The area was mountainous, rugged, and thickly forested. Their failure to find Ed would lead to an interesting and unpleasant encounter between a member of the Yavapai County Forest Patrol and the Find Me and AZSTAR volunteers in less than two weeks.

May Day, May 1st, is an international holiday, but Rhonda Younger had no cause to celebrate when she met with Detective Jack Nelson of the Phoenix Police Department. What he told her was obvious, but nonetheless painful. Ed was an adult and capable of making adult decisions, including the decision to just go away. Additionally, there was no evidence of foul play, so there was very little any police department could or would do. Nelson filed missing person report #60829473 – a long shot at best. The report was little more than a formality, meaning only that if Ed was picked up by some police authority they would see that a report had been filed. She understood his position and his reasoning, but that understanding did nothing to calm her fears. Ed was not someone who would just disappear.

Those fears were heightened on May 3rd when she was notified that Ed's truck had been found and that she should contact Detective John McDermitt with the Yavapai County Sheriff's Office in Prescott, AZ. McDermitt told her that he had filed a report of the abandoned vehicle and had listed the case as a missing person under report #06015852. That was all that he could really do, he said. Rhonda again heard the familiar story. Ed was an adult. There was no indication of foul play. The sheriff's office could do no more.

The reader should make note of this all too common situation. Police authorities throughout the country handle missing person cases in exactly the same manner. You would be amazed and perhaps shocked to learn the extent of effort required to get a police department to investigate these type of cases. It's understandable, but for the families and friends involved it's at best frustrating. It can be heart-breaking.

The Psychics Go to Work

Rhonda understood and appreciated the position of the authorities, but that did nothing to help locate her fiancée. She, like so many others, realized she had to take matters into her own hands and began searching the Internet for resources. She found a group in Arizona called AZSTAR (Arizona Search, Track and Rescue), the sister organization to Find Me. Rhonda contacted the leader of the organization, Kristi Smith, on May 4th. Smith immediately contacted Find Me director Kelly Snyder who immediately called Rhonda. He asked for some basic information: Ed's biography, a current photo, and the circumstances surrounding his disappearance. Rhonda also wanted a face-to-face meeting the following day. Snyder agreed and asked that she bring a sample of Ed's clothing, preferably a hat or jacket that would still have his scent. AZSTAR uses scent dogs, tracking dogs and cadaver dogs. In cases in which an individual has been missing for a short time there is always the possibility that his or her scent will be fresh enough for the dogs to sense, track andlead them to the subject of the search.

Snyder met with Rhonda, Brenda and Joel on May 5th. Rhonda brought a recent photo and some basic information necessary for some of the psychics to work with such as Ed's time of birth, place of birth and date of birth. She also provided additional information about Ed's last known activities so a time line could be established. Such information is valuable to some of the psychics because it helps establish that they are connecting to the right individual during their meditations. Few people realize it, but "crossed wires" are not uncommon in psychic investigation. A psychic can be looking for "Fred" in Texas, but can easily develop information about "Ginger" in North Dakota. A proper time line and sequence of events helps the psychic investigators make sure they are on the right trail.

May 9, 2006 – Find Me psychics were alerted to Ed Hatfield's disappearance and were requested to file their reports immediately. In most cases by the time the authorities bring in Find Me the case has become a cold case. Sadly, instead of looking for a living human being, the skills of these vetted psychics are therefore charged with finding human remains. Police and other authorities concerned with finding missing persons should begin to think of using vetted psychics as first responders instead of last chances. The time line between filing a missing person report and contacting a psychic group can be the difference between life and death.

As with the general public, law enforcement personnel have mixed feelings about psychic abilities and in working with psychics to find missing persons. To many psychics the attitude represents a last resort scenario. "Hell, we've tried everything else; we might as well call in those psychics." In Ed's case there was no real sense of urgency. After all, there was no indication of foul play. Any number of scenarios were possible:

He could be an adult run-away.

He could have been injured and placed unconscious in a hospital.

He could be on a binge and holed up in some motel room.

He could be getting away from it all at some camp site in the mountains.

He could be… anywhere.

The Find Me psychics began their work. Some meditated. Some sought direct contact with Ed or Ed's spirit. Others read Tarot cards, worked with pendulum dousing, used remote viewing techniques, began dreaming, consulted astrology charts and using other disciplines to find the missing man. Each gave freely of his or her time and talents knowing that there would be no financial reward and no individual glory for the effort.

The psychics' reports began coming in soon. As always, some turned out to be way off, some were close, and, as always, some proved to be right on target.

"I kept getting the message through about depression or sadness within him at the time a lot of stress around him, on a work level… (his body) is at least 20 minutes away from the site of the car, possibly even if one is walking. It is off a really major highway where the trees are short and windblown and very sandy rocky areas…"

"I feel Edward will be found deceased."

"Deceased. Saw fatal stab wound to Edward's solar plexus/chest area. Random robbery/homicide."

"Dead, shot."

No psychic gets a complete picture of an event. Regardless of portrayals in novels, television and motion pictures, generally a psychic will get only a piece of the puzzle - an image, a sound, a smell, a color, a feeling or some obscure clue. Some get more than others and sometimes they get nothing at all. Whatever they get or do not get, each member is required to file a report on the case. The concept behind Find Me is that the more pieces of the puzzle you get the better your chances of solving the mystery. Here are some of the clues received.

- Ed was alive.
- Ed had hitched a ride to Las Vegas.
- He was in a bar in Camp Verde.
- He was hiding out in Camp Verde
- Ed had been murdered by two men who had robbed him.
- He was deceased, above Rattlesnake Canyon and his body exposed to the elements.
- Ed was deceased and his body could be found approximately 300 yards Southeast of where his truck had been found.

- He was within a 15 minute walk Southeast of where his truck had been found.

Right or wrong, the information can be valuable to the psychics. This may be challenging for some to understand, but psychics can be right and wrong at the same time. The information a psychic receives is accurate. But that information must be interpreted and if there are inaccuracies that is where the inaccuracies show up. That is where things can go wrong. Feedback on these cases is essential because it allows the psychics to hone their skills and improve their abilities to accurately interpret the messages received. In the case of Ed Hatfield, a number of psychics had psychic hits on Camp Verde. The town is a considerable distance from where Ed disappeared, yet this is where the Sheriff's department impound facility is located. Ed's truck was in Camp Verde.

Psychic phenomena is not and cannot be an exact science. It is certainly not accurate every time a psychic works a case. One of the major goals of Find Me is to establish a more precise system of research and interpretation so as to make fewer and fewer errors. Achieving this goal will inevitably lead to providing police authorities and rescue groups with more accurate information which will make them more inclined to work with a psychic group to assist in their investigations. Instead of being a court of last resort the psychics want to be put at the top of the list on the resources call sheet.

In criminal cases and certainly in missing person cases, wouldn't you want the authorities to use *every* resource available?

Smith contacted Snyder on May 9th saying AZSTAR wanted to conduct a search the following morning in the area where Ed's truck was found. She was concerned that Ed's trail would be growing cold. Scent can linger, but it can also move, floating on the wind.

A victim's scent can easily jump from one hill top to another or down one side of a canyon and up the other. It can also dissipate. If

Ed were to be found alive, a rapidly dimming hope, immediate action was necessary.

Find Me Members Become "Ground pounders"

Snyder contacted Find Me member Dan Baldwin who readily agreed to join in the onsite search. An avid hiker, Baldwin believed his wilderness experience could be an asset to the AZSTAR efforts as a "ground pounder," a member of a search team. Baldwin practices pendulum dowsing and his research placed Ed on the side of Rattlesnake Canyon a mile or so southwest of where the truck had been found. Snyder and Baldwin met Smith and the members of AZSTAR on May 10th at an exit just of I-17. The time was 6:30 a.m. and the sun was already high in the sky. They quickly moved to the official search site at mile marker #310 at approximately 7 a.m. The psychics had done their work, but from that moment on this was an AZSTAR operation.

AZSTAR isn't a group of people who just get together to look for missing persons. The organization is well-organized, well-trained, well-managed and thoroughly professional in attitude and practice. The process for conducting a search is very technical and each member must be prepared for a long and potentially dangerous search. The process begins with equipment checks, radio checks, cell phone checks, mobile GPS system checks, making sure there is enough food and water for the searchers and for the scent, tracker and cadaver dogs. Areas are searched according to a grid system laid out on a map of the area. Teams are assigned numbers (Team #1, Team #2 and so on) and searches are conducted one grid at a time. Only after a grid has been cleared does the team move on to the next. It is a slow and methodical process, but a thorough one. That day four teams were involved, each team consisting of a dog, a dog handler and one support person responsible for maintaining radio contact, monitoring GPS coordinates, and to keep the team on track. Baldwin accompanied Team #1 which picked up a scent west across the Interstate. Team #2 searched northeast of the base camp, Team #3 searched a grid southeast of base camp, and Team #4 searched a grid due south.

The teams moved out at approximately 8:15 a.m. The temperature was 65 degrees Fahrenheit, excellent for conducting a search. Temperatures do not present a challenge until they reach 80 – 85 degrees. The wind was near zero. A search dog can catch a scent on the wind and follow it to its source. A lack of wind, however, is not detrimental to a search, just a bit more of a challenge because the dogs have to work harder. Each dog undergoes hundreds of hours of training before going on an official search, so they are trained for all climates, terrains and weather conditions.

By mid-morning the dogs were heating up and the teams were reporting a need for more and more frequent rest breaks. In such conditions dogs need about 15 – 20 minutes rest in shade and plenty of water. By 11 a.m. the heat had become such a challenge that Smith recalled the teams. They would return the following weekend to continue the search.

AZSTAR and Snyder and Baldwin from Find Me met at 4:30 a.m. on May 14th so that the teams could get an earlier start. The temperature was 55 degrees and spirits were high for a successful search. Snyder noted that they were searching on Mother's Day. Perhaps that would bring them good luck. Of course, "good" and "luck" are relative terms. Everyone met at the site of the previous command post and began the process of conducting another search. The first two teams set out the moment there was sufficient light, about 5:45 a.m. Baldwin noted that there were two prominent ridges overlooking Rattlesnake Canyon – about a quarter mile to the east and one about half a mile to the west. His pendulum reading had placed Ed further south, but Baldwin said, "If he's here, he'll be on that high point above the canyon." He didn't credit psychic ability for this judgment, only logic. If someone were to commit suicide (a feeling growing stronger throughout the searches) those were the loveliest spots with the best views. "That's where I'd do it," he said.

Team #1 headed out to search a grid northeast of the command post. Team #2 moved into a grid southeast. Snyder and Baldwin, perhaps sensing a successful search, remained at the command post to respond to any events as quickly as possible. At 7 a.m. Team #1 reported that they were on scent and had actually found footprints that appeared to be from cowboy boots. Ed Hatfield wore cowboy boots. The trail led uphill. Visual tracking was difficult because the Rattlesnake Canyon area is rocky and covered with tall grasses.

The tall grass took on added significance when Baldwin excused himself to answer "the call of nature." Out of sight of the command post he came upon a National Park Service sign reading "Rattlesnake Quiet Area." AZSTAR and Find Me were conducting a search in a rattlesnake preserve. You can imagine the excitement when he shared that news. By 7:20 Team #1 reported that they had lost the scent and were heading back to where they had found the boot prints and where the scent had been strongest for their dogs. At 8:10 they reported that they were back on scent and headed southeast. The dog's nose was pointed up in the air and not on the ground. The handler believed their reaction indicated that the scent was further up the mountain or coming from a hillside several hundred yards away. Scent can present challenges even for the most experienced dog team. It can hover in one spot or move around. The scent of a missing person can be a considerable distance from the person who made it. That's why a precise grid search is so important.

Team #1 remained in constant contact with the command post as they climbed the mountain. Clearly the search dog was on Ed's scent, but where was Ed? The team returned to the area they had previously searched, but could see nothing. Still, the dog was on to something. That's when one of the searchers looked up.

She saw the decomposing body of Ed Hatfield, still tied to the pine tree overlooking the canyon. His last view, his last sundown must have been spectacular. The team could see a small pile of cigarettes and an empty bottle of whiskey at the base of the tree. Unseen, but later found was his .38 revolver. Ed had shot himself in the head.

The call "we have a code" came in at 8:45, meaning the team had located the subject of the search and that the subject was deceased. Snyder, Smith and Baldwin immediately headed to the site. The other teams were recalled and told to remain at the command post.

Snyder, Smith and Baldwin arrived at the site at 9:10 and immediately began helping the AZSTAR team set up a perimeter. The area was now officially a crime scene and legal protocol was required.

The area immediately surrounding Ed's body was cordoned off with the yellow crime scene tape familiar to viewers of police dramas. Find Me and AZSTAR understand, respect and adhere to protocol. This is crucial in every discovery of a missing person. Potential evidence, which may be required in court, can be disturbed. The searchers had done their job and they had done it well. Now the situation was a police matter. The team's responsibility was to avoid disturbing the scene, to notify the appropriate authority, to protect the scene and then turn it over to the proper authority. The teams are so well trained that they walk out of the crime scene in the same steps they made getting in to it just to avoid any chance of crime scene contamination.

The Yavapai County Sheriff's Office had been notified in advance that a search would be conducted, so they were prepared to answer Snyder's call. Detective Frank Bararo and a uniformed Yavapai officer arrived at 10:30. Their awareness of the situation made the transfer of the crime scene brief and easy and without any undue complications.

Find Me and AZSTAR operate according to a strict set of guidelines so as to avoid miscommunication, delaying the legal process, or creating jurisdictional issues between agencies. It is a serious responsibility taken very seriously and the volunteers have earned high marks from law enforcement agencies for their professionalism.

Some of Ed's family members and a couple of friends who had come down from North Carolina to pass out missing person leaflets were waiting at the command post. Baldwin says their faces reflected a sad "we know better, but we still hope" look. Obviously, they were not permitted to go to the crime scene. Ed had shot himself in the head and had been exposed to the elements for nearly two weeks. No one should be remembered in that condition.

No Thanks for All Your Hard Work

After the crime scene had been turned over to Yavapai County authorities, Smith conducted a debriefing of all the teams. This is customary. Each team describes its search and notes any positive or negative aspects of that search. Topics can include dog performance, equipment malfunctions, radio communication problems, challenges encountered, recommendations for improvements to be incorporated into the next search and so on. The goal is continuing improvement.

Snyder made a similar report from the psychic perspective. "I think the two groups have worked well together. We've made our case for psychic research teams combining talents with on-the-ground search teams. Finding Ed Hatfield has proven our point and then some," he said.

You would think that police authorities would appreciate the efforts of volunteer groups such as Find Me and AZSTAR, volunteers who give up an incredible amount of time and energy and who often risk their health and occasionally their lives to help others. This isn't always the case. During the debriefing several Yavapai County Forest

Patrol vehicles arrived. Two of the officers entered the command post and demanded to know what was going on. They were informed of the situation, the arrangements with the proper authorities, the finding of Ed Hatfield and the handoff of the crime scene to the proper authorities.

As they departed another Forest Patrol vehicle arrived and the officers held a brief discussion among themselves. The late arrival, a female officer, entered the command post and proceeded to read the riot act to the assembled volunteers. She listed the various laws the two groups had broken and the violations of protocol they had committed. None of her complaints were true. Snyder had been working with the Yavapai County Sheriff's Office from the beginning. He had gone through the proper channels and had kept the office informed of all activities related to the case. Believing that the officer was venting her frustration over the fact that Find Me and AZSTAR had found Ed when her organization had failed in a similar attempt, Snyder and Smith let her ramble on. For the record AZSTAR had the right to conduct searches anywhere provided they have permission to be on the location and the responsible police authority is informed. In this case the search was conducted with the authority of Officer McDermitt and of Roy Armstrong, the Forest Service Patrol supervisor for the district. Not one to let unprofessional behavior go unchallenged, Snyder informed the Yavapai County Sheriff's Office of the incident on May 15. His follow up letter was well received and they extended their regrets over the incident and stated that the situation would be addressed. They also stated their appreciation for the volunteer efforts and that the groups would find continued support from their office. A follow-up report on the search was subsequently provided to the Yavapai County Sheriff's Office. This is standard procedure with Find Me and AZSTAR. The detailed report includes a description of each grid search, the number of teams, the number of dogs participating,

GPS coordinates, times and dates of every action performed by the group, names of every search team and any other pertinent information. Generally, psychic investigators have little or no experience with correct protocol. That's why psychic detecting groups should include a number of retired law enforcement officers among their members. Not only can they "talk the talk" of the police, and government investigators, they can make sure that proper protocol is followed at all times.

* * *

There is a sad postscript to Ed Hatfield's sad story. He had killed himself primarily due to depression over his inability to find work in Phoenix. Had he stayed at Joel and Brenda's home a few days longer he would have been around to answer an important phone call, a message that was left on their answer machine. The call came from a construction company. Ed got the job.

"None of us will ever accomplish anything excellent or commanding except when he listens to this whisper which is heard by him alone."

~Ralph Waldo Emerson

Chapter Two: Finding the Psychic Connection

Dear Kelly,

On November 18, 2012, the La Plata County Sheriff's Office began an investigation into the disappearance of 13 year old Dylan Nicholas Redwine, who traveled from Monument, Colorado to visit his father in the Vallecito Lake area for Thanksgiving break. Dylan's search intensified as winter rapidly emerged in this cozy mountain community. Dylan's family, as well as law enforcement, and hundreds of members from the community, searched tirelessly around the Vallecito Lake area, as well as the rest of La Plata County, the state of Colorado and elsewhere; but to no avail.

I received a call from Kelly Snyder, founder of the organization, "Find Me", within a few weeks of the investigation. Kelly informed me about Find Me, and about the unique services the extraordinary members of his team have to offer. He said Find Me specializes in missing persons. His group of dedicated and selfless associates was comprised of K-9 search dogs and dog handlers, retired and active duty law enforcement, psychics, hand-writing experts, and the list goes on. Kelly relayed to me that Find Me is a non-profit organization, and his services were free.

Our investigation was officially ruled a homicide. The discovery of Dylan's remains was devastating, and "bitter-sweet" as described by Dylan's older brother, Cory Redwine, and the rest of the family. They will never have to wonder what happen to Dylan, because of the aid and assistance from Find Me; the mystery of where Dylan is has ended, leaving open a new chapter in this ongoing investigation.

The search on Middle Mountain for more remains and evidence continued into late 2013. Again, members of Find Me answered the call and assisted with another arduous search of the San Juan National Forest. The search for more of Dylan continues to date, and Find Me has expressed their eagerness to return to La Plata County, Colorado in the spring of 2014.

No words can express my deep appreciation and gratitude to the dedicated and passionate members of Find Me who volunteered to take the time out of their busy lives without hesitation or reservation, to travel to rural Colorado on their own expense to help a family desperate for answers, and to provide my agency their elite special training and services. We are forever in their debt.
Sgt. Investigator Tom Cowing, La Plata County, (Colorado) Sheriff's Office

Time to Kick In a Few Doors

The founding of the Find Me organization is an interesting story and for those who are interested in forming a psychic detecting group it is highly illustrative.

"If there's a missing kid on the other side of the door, I'm not going to waste time filling out reports and waiting for instructions; I'm kicking the damn door in and I'll worry about reports after the rescue," says Kelly Snyder, founder of Find Me.

The words sum up the group's philosophy when called to action: take action. Prior to retirement from the Drug Enforcement Administration (DEA) Snyder could not see himself allowing his skills, experience and know how go to waste. He felt a powerful need to improve the lives of children in some capacity. He eventually met with a fellow retired agent who introduced him to the National Center for Missing and Exploited Children (NCMEC) and everything seemed to fall right into place. It was an ideal match between the needs of an important organization and the talents of a man dedicated to its stated goals.

The NCMEC was a good group, but he felt their pace was slow. He was used to a "There are the bad guys; let's get 'em now." Six months passed before he got his first case. Although that case was successfully resolved, ten months passed before he received another assignment. The U.S. Department of Justice estimates that 700,000 children go missing every year in the United States. Of the 4,000 persons who go missing every day, nearly 2,000 of them are kids. He decided to leave NCME and create his own group to find as many of those missing children as possible and, hopefully, at a faster pace.

He wondered if there were any alternative measures that could be employed to even the playing field between criminal and cop. "Is there something else we could do? Are there avenues we haven't explored? Am I missing something?"

Criminals always have the upper hand in committing crimes. They select when, where and how to attack there victims. And even in cases of unplanned violence, the odds favor an escape specifically because the act is so unexpected. Generally, criminals have an escape plan, which gives them element of surprise and the advantage of where they will abduct, sexually assault the child and in most cases murder and dispose of the body. This whole process normally takes the pedophile about four hours, not exactly sufficient time for the police to find and capture the perpetrator and save the child. The Amber Alert System is a major plus in leveling the playing field, but it assumes the police know who took the child and have a suspect and vehicle description. Sadly, this is not always the case.

The First Responder System is also very good, but even in the best of systems time is the enemy. The police have to arrive at the scene, conduct an investigation, complete interviews, and develop a plan of action – even if that plan has to be developed on-the run. Time favors the guilty. Each passing moment brings the victim more pain and terror and closer to a tragic and often agonizing death.

A tracking canine is a significant plus, but in most police departments it's a luxury and they usually don't have an available canine and in some cases no canine at all. Requesting help from other police department canine units is normal procedure, but valuable time is lost making arrangements. While all this is going on, the young and innocent victim is at best suffering fear and confusion or far too often terror, torture and worse.

Finding the Find Me Concept

Snyder wondered if psychics could help in child abduction cases. A skeptic, he also wanted to know if the psychic phenomenon was real. As a retired cop with decades of experience, he was aware of "cop instinct" and "gut feelings" that psychics say are merely other terms for psychic awareness. Also, he wasn't afraid to try new techniques. He investigated psychics and eventually met one who told him two important facts: psychic phenomena is real, but is not always accurate. The best description provided by the psychic was "sometimes it works and sometimes it doesn't." Just like everyone else on the planet, psychics have good days and they have bad days. As

Baldwin frequently says, "A psychic with a bad head cold isn't going to have a good day gazing into the void."

Snyder's commitment to finding missing children outweighed his skepticism about psychic phenomena. Even if psychic skills worked only 35-50 percent of the time investigators would be well ahead of the game and police authorities and search and rescue teams would have an added advantage. Baldwin says, "If you could do something that would give you a 35 – 50 percent better chance at the gaming tables in Las Vegas, wouldn't you take it? Then why wouldn't you up your odds the same way in finding a missing loved one?"

Employing psychic detecting techniques would also provide a better shot at rescue and survival of the missing. The combination of an open mind, the desire to find missing children, and the frustration of working through a bureaucracy provided the motivation and ultimately the drive to move forward with the idea.

Growing Pains

"If you're here for a share of reward money or for personal glory, you're in the wrong place." Snyder let prospective members know that participation in the group would be solely for the benefit of victims and their families. No one in what would become Find Me would use a tragedy for personal gain.

The evolution of the group was very slow. Initially there were only a few psychics in the group and the cases were selected at random. Baldwin was there from the inception and is considered an inaugural member. Those psychics contacted other psychics and little by little the group started to grow.

As with all new organizations there were numerous challenges. The psychics who were interested in personal glory or a shot at reward money left quickly. From its inception Find Me has never sought or accepted reward money from families. Publicity efforts were targeted towards solving cases and not to promote any one person or group of persons within the organization. Some new members proved to be psychic in name only. Then there were those who had ego problems and who wanted to make changes that would benefit them personally, but not necessarily the group or the cause. They also left when their wishes/demands were not well received. Above all, the needs of the victims and their families were always most important and any volunteer who did not understand or couldn't function under those guidelines was encouraged to volunteer somewhere else. These are important considerations for those people considering forming a psychic detecting group. It is very likely similar challenges will arise.

Naturally, Snyder encountered psychics who thought they were the best in the world. One in particular that continually made the statement "I am 92 percent accurate," but this individual would never document her work. She only wanted to pass on information verbally. In other words, despite being "92 percent accurate" she refused to go on the record. Another psychic bragged once too often about her 80 percent accuracy rate. Snyder snapped, "Then why are you sending me only the other 20 percent?" She, like many others who followed, weren't right for the group. That's one of the reasons for running a thorough background check on each prospective member. It's a good idea, also, to require new members to work for a year in probationary status before earning full membership.

Find Me continued to make changes, establish guidelines and tighten up the procedures for accepting new members. From the outset the organization wanted to present itself to families and authorities as a group of professionals. The group established a questionnaire and guidelines so that all potential members could see what was expected of them. The guidelines were very simple, just do the best you can, always report on every case positive or negative and be committed to the group for however long you are a member.

And never forget that the needs of the victim and the families are always paramount.

Taking Action

As with the larger community Find Me serves, its members embrace a wide range of religious and faith-based beliefs, but they held a strong belief that a higher power would provide cases and that the group should only take case requested by family/friends or from law enforcement. There was never a desire to become the ambulance chaser of the psychic world. Snyder would review a case and then telephone the law enforcement detectives in charge to see if they would accept psychic help. The police would agree to accept the information, but without feedback it was very difficult to determine if they actually acted on that information. The group had to rely on the families, the internet and news reports keep track of how a given investigation was progressing.

Find Me psychics have skills that run the gamut: card reading, intuitives, clairvoyants, clairaudients, mediums, pendulum dowsers, remote viewers, forensic astrology and others. Additionally, they began to add other, non-psychics skills such as court-recognized handwriting analysts, linguists, forensic facial reconstruction experts, and a group of pilots volunteered their time and aircraft to act as an air wing.

The lack of feedback from law enforcement proved to be an ongoing challenge. It's understandable to the psychics, but nonetheless frustrating. Belief in the value of psychic detecting varies from full acceptance to skepticism to outright hostility depending on the organization and the personnel within. And, of course, evidence discovered by psychics isn't exactly welcomed in court.

"And just how did you discover the body, officer?"

"Well, this lady who talks to dead people told us..."

"What!"

"And this guy who swings a rock on a swing said the same thing, so..."

"Next witness!"

Still, the word got out and families and friends and police departments started emailing and asking for help. Early on Find Me received a request from a local Arizona family looking for a twin brother, Fred, who had medical issues. Upon their return from a weekend get-a-way trip they arrived at an empty house. Fred was nowhere to be seen and there were no clues left to indicate where he had gone. The police department did not help the family other than to file a report that he was missing. They knew he had a medical condition, but looking for missing adults in not a priority or requirement and in most cases it takes an "act of Congress" to even get them to file a missing person report., "It's incredibly frustrating. They'll accept sight-unseen an anonymous tip over the telephone, but are skeptical when a bunch of talented people with a provable track record offer solid information," said one of the members.

One of the goals of Find Me is to convince police and related authorities that vetted psychics should be considered a first-responder. "Bring us in right away and you'll dramatically increase your chances of a successful investigation," Snyder says.

FINDING CHALLENGES

It's SOP (standard operating procedure) in almost every city, county and state in the USA that the police will not look for an adult, unless there are extenuating circumstances such as a suicide note, a letter saying that he or she is going to kill someone and blow up buildings, or something along those lines. The situations must be something that will require the police to look for the individual to prevent a crime. The disappearance, at least initially, isn't considered a crime. Adults walk away from their jobs, families and responsibilities all the time. The policy is also SOP in the case of a missing child over the age of 12. The authorities will usually at least file the report, but in almost all cases they label the missing kid as an endangered runaway. These procedures are understandable, but tragic. A lot of people fall through the cracks and far too many of them are never seen or heard from again.

The authorities on any given case must operate according to the realities of the situation. Still, those realities are to say the least frustrating. If you want to see how most children are labeled go to www.ncmec.org pick your state and start clicking on the photos. You will be shocked at how many are categorized as "endangered runaways" or "parental abduction." Once again, the parents have to provide something that will encourage an investigation, otherwise they put them in the National Criminal Information Center (NCIC) as a BOLO (Be On the Look Out), report them missing to NCMEC, and then walk away. They become missing and, except for the immediate family, forgotten. In most police departments they may provide a poster with photo of a missing child or adult at roll call or during a squad briefing, but these actions are not a requirement.

Here are some statistics to ponder: in 2006 there were 836, 131 missing person records entered in the NCIC. Medical examiners in 2006 reported approximately 4,400 of unidentified human remains. Even after their investigation to identify the bodies, there still remained an average of 1000 that are never identified each year.

Until legislation changes the landscape of how police operate missing person cases, the public will get little or no help and the hands of the police will continue to be tied. You can't be upset if the law and rules don't allow for the police to assist you. Virtually every police officer the group has dealt with believes in doing the right thing by all citizens, but most street cops are not running the show.

They report to management and management reports to the Chief and the Chief reports to the Mayor and so on and so on.

* * *

Dear Kelly,

My family wished to express our appreciation for the support and commitment you and the Find Me group gave us during the search for our daughter. Meeting with you and your group, feeling the concern and caring expressed, helped us through a difficult time in our lives. The ending of the search was not what we had hoped for, but we were able to bring Marcy home and we are grateful to have her with us once again.

Sincerely,

Lynda Randolph

* * *

PSYCHIC INTERPRETATION

Psychic information is solid information. The problem in working with that information is interpreting the meaning. The psychic's personal world view, set of experiences, belief system and so on can easily color the interpretation and even lead to misinterpretation. All psychics have their own techniques of receiving information and many function well in multiple categories. For example, some psychics work with a spirit guide or multiple guides who helps them ferret out clues and locations. These guides often take on a human appearance. As one psychic reported, "The guide in this reading was a white slender man, a doctor, with wireframe glasses. I feel it was through him that this information came. He wore a white doctor's coat with blue writing on it."

The psychic information may be gathered by dowsing with a

string and piece of stone, tarot cards, dreaming, or remote viewing where the person sees the crime being committed either by watching it from a distance, watching it through the eyes of the suspect or even scarier, experiencing the event as the victim. Depending on the individual person's gifts, psychics can hear things, see things, taste or smell things, talk to the deceased, channel the deceased, talk to spirit guides, dream about what and how the crime or disappearance occurred. In a recent case one of the psychics actually heard the threats uttered by a kidnapper against his victim.

"You must be proactive or you could die," he said.

In another case the psychic actually experienced the kidnapping and murder of a victim from that victim's perspective. The report included, "They told me to run and I did, then they shot me in the back of my leg and then came out where I fell and then shot me in the chest. It was quick more or less. Tell my daughter I'm sorry, she always said I had a soft heart and I guess this time I tried to help the wrong guy."

Sometimes interaction with those on the other side can become physical. One of our psychics examined a photo of a missing person and, "When I picked up her photo, she slapped it out of my hand. We had been talking about her boyfriend and his role in things. I kept hearing her say, 'We have it all wrong regarding her boyfriend.'" Regardless of how these abilities materialize, the end result is that the psychic has to determine the meaning of the symbols, words, thoughts, and sensory impressions. Some psychics experience certain physical reactions to their readings. One report noted, "There is a buzzing energy coming from the pictures, usually that means someone is determined." This process is where the truth can become fiction. If the psychic sees the word "Barclay" does that mean it's the suspects last name, the street he/she lives on, the town where the suspect lives or where the missing person can be located. "Barclay" was a character in *Star Trek – The Next Generation.* Does the clue refer to the television series, space travel, engineering or even the actor who played the role of Barclay?

Baldwin says, "The information is always right; but the meaning can be obscure and our interpretation can be off track." There are so many variables and it takes months/years of practice for the psychics to evaluate over and over what symbols and words mean in the context of their meditation. One of the real strengths of working with a group of psychics is that the various images, perhaps meaning little or nothing to the individual psychic, may contribute to a very precise solution to a problem when all the bits and pieces are put together. A bunch of seemingly unrelated bits of information and impressions can form a coherent picture when assembled.

There are several scientific studies being conducted throughout the world about psychic phenomena and these studies are attempting to determine if there is a way to create a system to refine the process of interpretation. Some Find Me psychics are in the forefront of these investigations. The significance of these studies is to bring about an understandable methodology or at minimum an opportunity to fine tune the process. This will take years, but at least the projects are underway. Understand that the psychic phenomenon exists. The problem with it is the percentage of correct answers versus incorrect answers is about 35-50 percent correct and the rest undetermined, but not necessarily incorrect. By this we mean, the answer may be there (Barclay) but what is Barclay?

Chris Robinson, an extremely talented and accurate psychic England, is a good example of how psychics face and overcome this challenge. He has been cataloging his dreams for nearly 20 years. He now knows with total certainty that when he dreams of dogs, the dogs mean criminal/suspect/terrorist and so on. Snow means something will happen soon on that same context such as a crime, a bombing, or a bank robbery. A blizzard means whatever is going to happen is eminent. He keeps a log of every dream and when he is able to validate what he sees, he makes a notation in his logbook of what he saw and what actually happened. Every psychic should be so diligent with the study of his or her skills.

Recording information and comparing research vs. results can only enhance the psychic's abilities. The official Find Me report each member uses, provides just such a mechanism. People outside the world of psychic investigations often have a distorted view of the process and its effects on the practitioner. Psychics know the reality and that's often far from what is presented in television and films. Exploring a crime hundreds or thousands of miles away in the comfort of one's home or office may seem a safe and secure procedure and for most investigators that's true. However, sometimes the crime and/or the criminals involved can have a decidedly unpleasant or even a negative impact on the investigator.

Baldwin says his pendulum dowsing is virtually free of emotion. The process involves the movement of a handheld weight on a string. The dowser gets yes/no answers depending on the direction of the pendulum's swing. There are no visions, impressions, or sensations involved in the process – usually. Baldwin says, "We were working the case of a missing infant in Europe. I held my pendulum and asked my standard first question. 'Is this missing person physically alive?' Immediately and without warning I broke down and wept. It was an extremely emotional, uncontrollable and sad experience. They found the child's body later that day."

Another investigator on a different case had a far more intense experience. She wrote, "I won't be submitting a report for this case. I was working on it on Thursday and decided to go downstairs to get a glass of water. I saw this flash out of the corner of my eye, then I felt something push really hard on my back. Me feet flew up, but I had my hand on the rail, so the only thing that I hurt was my ass because that's what landed on never had a spirit attack me before. I didn't' even think they could. I don't think it was (name of victim deleted), but something else that came through with him. I also the stairs first. I've had fingernail marks on my back that lasted until yesterday. Made me a little nervous about contacting him again. Still trying to figure out how this thing got through my guardians."

Anyone who wants to become involved in psychic work should realize that there are hazards. Personal physical, mental and emotional safety should be a major concern. As Baldwin says, "You can get hurt in this business and in more ways than one."

GPS

Beginning in 2007 Find Me adopted the use of GPS (Global Positioning System) coordinates to specifically pinpoint the location of missing persons and suspects. This step is highly recommended for any group that wants to work effectively with law enforcement and related agencies. It's a simple process. For example, Google earth provides GPS coordinates for the locations plotted on its maps. The investigator just marks the spot and reads the GPS coordinates right on the screen.

This use of GPS coordinates is the result of contacts with police authorities who often stated that the psychic information provided them was usually too generic to be of any real value to the investigations.

"The victim is near water."

"The victim is surrounded by trees."

"There are mountains in the distance."

"I see a concrete structure."

"The number two is important."

"I smell some kind of chemical."

That information is solid, but it leads – nowhere. How many

places on Earth have water, trees, or mountains in the distance, concrete structures and so on and so on? No matter how specific, the information is of little value in solving the crime. For example, if a psychic states that the victim is five miles northeast of the corner of 5th and Vine, that's pretty specific, right? Wrong. Unless you have an exact heading when you arrive at the five mile marker your search area could be as large as a ten mile square. Like a wedge of pie, the farther out you get from 5th and Vine, the larger becomes the territory to be searched.

Who can blame the authorities for saying, "Thanks, but no thanks." They need specific, actionable information.

That's why psychics are turning more and more to the use of GPS coordinates on their cases. Instead of "pinpointing" a target the size of a county, they're pinpointing a target the size of a football field or smaller. They want to send the authorities or search and rescue teams directly to a *specific* location. The psychics also use standard maps, topographic maps, Google Earth and other tools to fine tune their efforts. The goal is to reduce the size of a search area to a search area that can be realistically covered within a realistic timeframe by the authorities and/or search and rescue teams.

In a case in Arizona the use of GPS coordinates by a Find Me psychic, located the body of someone involved in a motor vehicle accident with an "error" of less than one foot. It should also be mentioned that some psychics can identify an area with landmarks, but that is still not as accurate as GPS coordinates. For example, Find Me was searching for a missing airplane. Eighteen of 26 members responding to the assignment identified a valley near Sedona, AZ. All GPS "hits" were within four to six miles of each other. Others psychics had "hits" within the same general area. Keep in mind this is coming from psychics all over the world who do not communicate with each other during their research process. They receive this information using their own particular skills. GPS coordinates were provided and the search continued. (What happened during that investigation is covered fully in a later chapter.)

One of the real challenges to using GPS coordinates is the actual terrain and that was especially true in this case. Find Me and AZ-STAR conducted searches by helicopter, fixed wing aircraft, and by ground in the targeted areas, but had to call of those searches due to the inaccessibility of the target sites. It was physically impossible for the search teams to go where they needed to go.

The reader should also note that no group of psychics will be in agreement 100 percent of the time. Six of the participating members in this search believe that the missing persons were alive and well and in a foreign country. They also provided a GPS coordinate, but as you would expect it becomes a little more difficult to search on foreign soil. Again, is the information received a matter of right or wrong or is it a matter of interpretation? Perhaps, the hits were the result of a psychic "crossed wire." Later research determined that years earlier one of the missing persons had crashed in a small plane near the alternate location indicated by these psychics.

* * *

Kelly,

I can't begin to tell you and the whole group what your service has meant to all of us that love Ed or begin to know what it would have been like to not have your group involved...After speaking with Kristi (AZ- Search & Rescue) and Kelly, (FIND ME) I went from frustration and feeling hopeless to having comfort that a group having the capability and resources cared and would do everything you could to find him. And you did. What heroes you all are.

Rhonda Younger

* * *

VETTED PSYCHIC DETECTIVES SHOULD BE FIRST RESPONDERS

One of the most frustrating challenges to psychic detective efforts is the "court of last resort" attitude expressed by law many enforcement authorities. "Well, nothing else has worked. We might as well give the psychics a try. What have we got to lose?" Unfortunately the call is usually weeks, months or even years after the person has gone missing. And what they lose is a great opportunity to get highly-trained, skilled and motivated people around the world working on the case while the case is still "hot."

Law enforcement and related agencies should realize the importance of contacting vetted psychic detectives the same day that the investigation is begun. A responsible group will never get in the way of law enforcement efforts, but it will start its own investigation to establish accurate information the authorities can put to use immediately. In most cases in an urgent matter like the disappearance of a child, the group can provide information within 24-48 hours. Time is critical, especially in a kidnapping case.

Arizona Search Track and Rescue (AZSTAR), Find Me's sister group, is always on stand-by and can react to requests within a few hours. They can have tracking dogs that will zero in on the scent from where the child/adult was last seen. It is extremely important to have dogs at the scene immediately and even if a police department has that capability with their own canine's and officers, the group can augment and complement the existing police canine corps. Serious psychics do not view their work as a hobby. This is serious business and in many cases is a matter of life and death. They respect law enforcement and honor the rules and regulations of a proper investigation.

The GPS information can provide your department with a useful tool that may identify the exact area in which a victim can be located. For example, Find Me was asked to help find a missing child in Colorado, a child feared dead and possibly murdered. The authorities were certain that the kid's remains were on a nearby mountain studded with old-growth forests. A mountain is a very big thing and to say the least challenging to search thoroughly. A number of psychics got "hits" on the mountain in question. Baldwin pinpointed a GPS location along a forest road near a specific hiking trail. Remains, later identified by DNA as belonging to the victim were found within 300 feet of that location. Reducing the search area from an entire mountain to a relatively small area can mean the difference between finding someone or some evidence and forever remaining in the dark. Coupled with psychic information, location and canine support there is a great chance the victim in a missing person case can be located before any harm is done or before an individual succumbs to the elements. In cold case research the psychic detectives groups can provide valuable information in locating remains, finding hidden evidence, and bringing the guilty party or parties to justice.

Authorities: think about that. Solid evidence that can be used in an investigation and in court, evidence that would in all likelihood have been scattered and lost forever, was found by a group of volunteer psychics supported by a volunteer search and rescue team. Police departments across the country are beginning to recognize the value of working with skilled and properly motivated psychics. Some believe in psychic abilities. Others are open or are becoming open to examining information regardless of the source. As one deputy sheriff put it, "I don't really believe in psychics, but your information is solid and I'll always act on any good lead." If police will just think of this phenomena as a tool to identify leads in their investigations they may see that it parallels investigative information they may have already. The key is to have an open mind and use the information just like you would if there was an anonymous caller with information. It's a lead that may potentially assist you in solving your case and more importantly saving a life at best and at worse bringing closure to a family of a missing loved one.

Generally, psychic detecting groups aren't in the "missionary" business. The organization isn't trying to make converts or believers or followers; they're too busy out in the field finding clues. They just want to find missing people and to solve crimes. To law enforcement agencies, they say with one voice, "You have to believe, but by all means put us to the test."

* * *

Kelly,

Thank you for all your help with our missing person in the City of Perry, Kansas. Our victim, Mr. Shawn Fowler, was found about an eighth of a mile from his home. He was found floating in the Delaware River within 100 feet of one of the GPS readings your team provided. He was found at approximately 13:45 hours on March 19, 2009. The river had been searched a couple of times by boat and scanner with no results the day prior to the body coming to the surface. Part of the information we concentrated on was the area around a submerged tree as predicted by one of your Team members. I have shared your Team efforts with Deputies, Firemen and Medical persons who assisted in the three month long search. Again THANK YOU ... THANKS TO THE TEAM !!!! The Family now has closure!

Respectfully,

Ramon C. Gonzalez, Jr. Police Chief

"As long as the day lasts, let's give it all we got."
~David O. McKay (Ralph Waldo Emerson)

Chapter Three: Marcy Randolph

Missing Arizona Plane

On Sunday, Sept. 24, 2006 at 10:43 a.m. a 1966 Cessna 182, tail #N2700Q (white with brown stripes), departed Deer Valley Airport near Phoenix with full fuel tanks. The craft soon disappeared. Although no flight plan was filed, it is believed the aircraft was headed for Sedona and was expected to return to Deer Valley that same afternoon or evening. A Civil Air Patrol search was begun the next day, but no trace of the plane or its two occupants was found.

There is a high probability that a radar contact that dropped off-screen approximately 9 NM SW of Sedona is the missing plane...

The pilot of N2700Q was William Westover, age 54, and his passenger was Diane Marcy Randolph, age 43. In less than three weeks members of Find Me were listening to their individual psychic voices and turning their attention to the magnificent, beautiful, rugged and dangerous red rock mountains of Sedona, Arizona.

Up in the Air. Under the Radar. Out of Sight

Sunday dawned a beautiful day, a "severe clear" day as some pilots describe it. From the air some of the nation's most striking country stretched on for mile after mile in beautiful detail unobscured by wind and rain, snow or sleet, clouds and fog. Marcy Randolph told her parents that she and her friend Bill were taking a short flight to enjoy brunch among the famous red rock country that surrounds Sedona. Her grandmother was scheduled for surgery later that day and

Marcy promised to be back no later than three p.m. The schedule would leave plenty of time for sightseeing along the way and even a pass over her parent's house in Munds Park a little northeast of Sedona.

What could be simpler?

Bill didn't file or need to file a flight plan because he was flying VFR or Visual Flight Rules. That means he would be "flying by the seat of his pants" using his senses for navigation rather than instruments. Flying IFR, flying using instrumentation, is more regimented and requires filing an exact flight plan to destination with the FAA. Both methods are common, so his plan to go VFR was nothing out of the ordinary.

Their small craft left Deer Valley and climbed to the desired altitude for a short and easy flight north. Flying in mountainous country carries with it the responsibility of being extra alert and cautious. The pilot must navigate through thermal updrafts, down drafts, wind shear, wind gusts and rapidly changing weather patterns. Heat, cold, humidity, speed, altitude and other factors must always be taken into consideration even on a clear day. A simple mistake or miscalculation can lead to tragedy. The FAA and nearby Luke AFB tracked Cessna N2700Q until 11:17 when it went below radar, apparently on final approach. Winds at Sedona Airport were gusting between 22 and 30 mph, which could have been tricky for Bill who only had about 450 hours flight time under his belt.

Marcy never showed up at the hospital for her grandmother's surgery and Bill never made it back to his family.

A Family's Anguish. A Father's Search.

By mid-afternoon, Phil and Lynda, Marcy's parents, knew something was wrong. Skipping out on an important hospital visit without any notice was not in her character. She wasn't answering her cell phone and calls to her friends revealed nothing as to her whereabouts. Bill Westover had not returned to his family either. The next day Phil called the Phoenix Police Department. Detective Amy Dillon was supportive, but said there was very little the department could do regarding a person missing out of their jurisdiction.

She did notify the Civil Air Patrol, the Department of Public Safety and the Sheriff's offices of Yavapai and Coconino Counties, the counties where the plane would most likely have gone down.

A crash was no longer a terrible possibility, but most likely a tragic reality.

In these situations the procedure is automatic and follows an established routine.

Phoenix PD, as the initiating agency, determined that Cessna N2700Q had not returned to Deer Valley Airport and apparently had not landed at another airport. The FAA was notified and the craft was officially listed as missing and presumed crashed. The authorities determined that the Civil Air Patrol (CAP) was the agency best prepared and with the best chances of locating the missing plane. Within two days CAP members were flying a grid pattern of approximately ten square miles from the Cessna's last known position. The two most likely areas for the crash were Sycamore and Oak Creek Canyons, positioned Northwest and Northeast respectively of the Sedona Airport. After two weeks and 252 flights, the CAP called off the search. It should be noted that the Sedona area is extremely popular with hunters, bird and wildlife watchers, photographers, four-wheel drive enthusiasts, mountain bikers, and hikers who crisscross the area in all seasons and in all weather. Additionally, the red rock country offers numerous jeep, helicopter, airplane and hot air balloon excursions. Yet there were no reports of a plane going down or sightings of wreckage – at least nothing the searchers were informed about at that time. Although beautiful, the canyons are treacherous and thickly wooded. An airplane could easily crash and slide beneath a virtually impenetrable forest canopy.

Phil Randolph had gotten the ball rolling, but he was not satisfied to sit and wait for reports to come in. His pilot's license had expired so he reapplied. Getting a new license is not like picking up a bicycle and starting up from where you left off. It's a long and challenging process, especially if you're desperate to use those skills to find a missing daughter. He pushed on and granted a new pilot's license and began his own intensive search. Phil was a dedicated and methodical investigator. He plotted and logged every search whether by ground or air and used GPS to document their efforts and to prevent duplication. He also took hundreds of photographs for review and study. He was leaving nothing to chance and was making every possible effort to make sure that every possibility of finding that airplane and his daughter would be covered and covered thoroughly. To say that his efforts were extensive is an understatement of grand proportions.

He methodically called the Bureau of Land Management, the U.S. Forest Service, Coconino County Search and Rescue, Yavapai County Search and Rescue, the State of Arizona and the U.S. Fish and Wildlife Services, hunters, fishermen, cyclists and hikers. He created missing person posters and a website.

One of the primary Find Me goals is to create enough awareness and credibility so that the group is brought into a missing person investigation as soon as possible, ideally the same day the case is opened. The earlier all avenues of exploration are brought into play, the more likely are the chances for a positive outcome. Eventually, Phil and Linda contacted a psychic which led to a connection with Find Me.

* * *

From: Kelly

To: (Find Me Personnel)

Sent: Tuesday, October 10, 2006 6:32 a.m.

Subject: Marcy Randolph

URGENT: PLEASE RESPOND IMMEDIATELY

Marcy Diane Randolph

DOB 12-8-62

Place of Birth: Phoenix, Arizona

TOB: 2:40 p.m.

Missing since 9-24-06: Departed Deer Valley Airport in small aircraft with Pilot William Westover

Kelly

The email call went out to the (at that time) 35 Find Me mediums, astrologers, forensic astrologers, remote viewers, precognitive dreamers, dowsers, clairvoyants, clairsentients, clairaudients, and any other type of "clair" you could think of.

The variety of skills employed is one of the major strengths of the group. More sights, sounds, feelings, impressions and bits of information mean a significantly better chance of solving the case at hand. *Find Me*, the first book about the group, explores in detail the different skills of certain members, their approach to finding missing persons, and tips and guidelines on how someone can develop his or her own psychic abilities. It is a great source of knowledge on how psychics arrive at predictions and how they use these methods to identify areas where we believe missing persons can be located.

Responses began coming in almost immediately.

"They are both deceased. Engine trouble. Lost radio contact. Plane went down west of Sedona, near the base of a mountain, in a heavy dense forestry area where there was no access whatsoever – no highway, no dirt road, no horse path or hiking trail. The only way they will be recovered is if a helicopter searches and spots them… Marcy briefly contacted me in spirit and says to tell her family she is fine and she loves them and that she will try to assist in them finding her…."

"I am not yet 100 percent but, I feel that they are in spirit and suddenly through plane engine fault or failure…I hope I am wrong, but I sensed at crash, and both dead. Please, GOD I pray I am wrong…"

"…they are both in the plane northwest of the Sedona airport and spirit was clear to show me they are located about 10-20 miles northwest of where the last search was conducted. The plane went down due to engine failure and that are both dead."

"…lots of green trees, red rock, plane is hidden under trees, still…not an area that is accessed. I believe both are dead…the plane is literally buried in the trees…"

"I also feel like Marcy is still not ready to be found. Shame and guilt of everyone knowing what she was doing, and the secretiveness behind it…"

"The plane is lying flat, not upside down…bodies are in the plane…I trust in divine timing, they will be found. I heard that it is in the Highest Good that their bodies be found and laid to rest for closure for the family left behind…"

"…gully area – plane is next to a sheer rock wall – very broken up – groundcover has grown up over the pieces…."

"…I see one older man approx. five miles to the east of the site, he heard impact but did not connect it to a plane crash…"

"As the plane headed towards Bear Canyon, at a location just east of Paulden, the pilot had a sudden medical event rendering him immediately incapable of controlling the plane… the plane is hidden in a ravine/below ground with only the white wing tip showing above ground level..."

Following what has become standard operating procedure, most of the psychics provided GPS coordinates with their reports.

POUNDING THE GROUND IN RED ROCK COUNTRY

Find Me participated in ten searches for Marcy Randolph, three on the ground and seven from the air. The group conducted one major search in conjunction with AZ-STAR. This search was in one of the most rugged terrains in the Sedona area. Schnebly Hill Vista is a rugged and winding road from Sedona east to Interstate 17 approximately ten miles away. It is a beautiful drive popular with tourists. The heavily forested canyons and steep cliffs on each side of the road discourage off-road travel and even hiking and horseback riding is challenging. As members of Find Me and AZ-STAR discovered, some of the terrain is impenetrable and in some cases dangerous.

The teams arrived in Sedona the day before the scheduled search. Some stayed in nearby motels while others camped out in a designated camping/parking area on the edge of town. The cost of food, beverage, fuel, and lodging was paid for by the individual volunteers on the search – as always. Everyone met several hours before sunup to coordinate the day's search.

A base camp was set up at one of the few wide turn-around areas on the road. In the field, AZ-STAR operates a converted trailer which is equipped with radios, survival and rescue gear, its own power source, and other equipment necessary to conduct search and rescue operations. Kelly Snyder, Dan Baldwin and Dave Crotchett (retired Kansas Highway Patrol officer) represented Find Me as ground pounders on this mission.

Many of the psychics had pegged this area as the spot where N2700Q would be found. GPS coordinates pinpointed a number of specific sites. Search grids were established and several teams set out.

The process was methodical and radio and/or telephone contact with base camp was maintained at all times. Once an area was cleared, the team would move on to the next assigned grid.

Unless someone has participated in a search and rescue mission through tough terrain it is hard to imagine just how challenging and dangerous the effort can be. For example, one member of AZ-STAR was scrambling up a steep canyon when the loose rock beneath his feet gave way. He slid down the canyon face, landing on a narrow ledge above a sheer drop off. Had he continued the fall, he would have been seriously injured or worse. Some of the teams struggled until continued searching became physically impossible. Certain grid areas could only be entered by airlifting team members in by helicopter and even that would have proven potentially hazardous to the searchers and the flight crew. Obviously, searchers in or approaching such areas were called back.

At the end of an exhausting day, the searchers had not found the plane or any sign of a crash. The best that could be said, which is saying a lot, is that large areas of potential crash sites had been eliminated. Such information is valuable and contributes to the effort by narrowing the overall search area.

Dream a Little Nightmare for Me

One of the long term members of Find Me is Chris Robinson, a precognitive dreamer from England. He is well-known throughout the world and has a psychic record that is phenomenal. Robinson has been written up in numerous newspapers, magazines and books and is the subject of a number of documentaries and scientific studies. He has also served as a government consultant on anti-terrorism issues.

Robinson's skill is dreaming. He devoted years of personal research to develop his skills and to learn, document and use the symbolism found in his dreams. Psychic dreamers know that their dreams are very personal. Anyone can pick up one of those dream interpretation books at any psychic bookstore to help understand dream symbolism. Robinson says those books are all right as far as they go – a very general guideline. He says that everyone has a different set of symbols and meanings for those symbols. For example, when Chris dreams about barking dogs he knows he is getting a message about terrorists or a terrorist attack. Other symbols in the dream help him hone in on the who, what, where, when and how. That same imagery might have an entirely different meaning, and probably will, for someone else. And it may have no serious meaning at all to another dreamer. To paraphrase the psychologist Sigmund Freud, "Sometimes a barking dog is just a barking dog." In his own dream state, Robinson knows the difference.

He was the subject of a documentary by October Films during the search for Marcy Randolph and the production company arranged a trip to Arizona to tape his participation in that case.

On May 25 Snyder, Chris and the October Films crew took the beautiful two-hour drive from Phoenix uphill to the red rocks of Sedona where they met Phil and Lynda. Using a hand held GPS system they drove to an open field and marked the spot where the plane went off radar, but would have been last seen if anyone had been in that location as the plane passed overhead. The area was an open field about 50 – 100 acres wide and it was easy to see that the plane had not crashed there or in the immediate vicinity. The questions were numerous. Did the plane actually fly over this spot? Did it veer left (west) toward Prescott? Did it veer right to Flagstaff or the Munds Park area? At that moment it was all guesswork and Find Me doesn't like to deal in guesses.

The investigation continued for most of the next week. One day they flew a predetermined route that might match the route of the missing plane. They flew over the valleys and mountains of Sedona and realized that if the craft went down in either Oak Creek Canyon or Sycamore Canyon a search and recovery mission would be incredibly challenging. The terrain is beautiful, but dangerous to the extreme. For example, two days would be required to climb and traverse a tortuous route just to get into remote Sycamore Canyon.

The crevasses, caves, steep hills and sheer drop offs would require an intensive, exhausting and potentially hazardous effort by AZ-STAR and the volunteer ground pounders from Find Me. A small plane flying at 110 – 150 knots going into a downward spiral would be shattered into many small parts upon impact with the Earth. The best hope for searchers involved in a plane crash is fire, smoke and a debris field, but the canyons and thick tree growth significantly reduce the chances of a recognizable debris field.

Robinson provided solid clues, but at that time the location of the plane remained a mystery.

LOST AND FOUND

Marcy Randolph and William Westover were lost September 24, 2006. Cessna N2700Q was found April 19, 2009 northwest of Sedona in Loy Canyon, roughly ten miles from Schnebly Hill Road and the targeted search area.

So, were the psychics in error?

Clearly some were. For example, a small number of psychics believed that the couple was alive and well and hiding in a Gulf of California resort town catering to American tourists. The other members who "saw" the crash in such a small area off Schnebly Hill Vista were obviously sensing something. Perhaps they were dealing with a psychic crossed wire and were picking up on some other missing person or persons. The likelihood of another crashed aircraft in that area is unproven, but is certainly a possibility. Again, as with any investigation, the search is in large part a numbers game. The investigators look where they think their chances of solving the case are best. This is especially true when looking for an aircraft that can travel hundreds of miles in any direction.

What about the other psychics? Twenty-eight psychics reported that the aircraft could not be seen from the air because the forest canopy was so dense. They also stated that the plane had crashed in a "valley/ravine/crevasse in a mountain close to Sedona Airport." This is a perfect description of where N2700Q was found. Eighteen members pinpointed GPS coordinates that were within five miles of the crash site. Considering the vast search area, that is an amazing statistic. One member noted a GPS coordinate only 1 ½ mile from the crash site.

A sad postscript to this case is that the missing plane and its occupants could have been found months and possibly a year earlier. Records from the U.S. Forest Service showed that two hikers in the Loy Canyon area had spotted, photographed and reported smoke and fire the day of the crash. They were unaware of the cause of the fire and by the time the Forest Service investigated the area, the fire had burned out. The information was not entered into the system for several weeks where it fell through the cracks and was never connected with the crash.

The report was discovered by an investigator two years and seven months later. Aerial photos taken during those years were compared with the photo taken by the hikers and the probable crash site was located. On-the-ground searches by the hikers and Yavapai and Coconino County mountaineers quickly located the wreckage and the remains of its two passengers. Perhaps the information that some of the psychics picked up was correct – perhaps Marcy wasn't ready to be found until long after the crash.

Chris and the Bear

October Films was excited about the documentary on Robinson, but they wanted to give him a dry run. As a test of Robinson's abilities the company selected a number of items, enclosed them in a box and challenged him to dream on and name the items. He did, dreaming of a bear, a circle, the number 121 and several other items. When the box was opened it contained a figure of a bear connected by a chain to a circle. Robinson felt that the three items had a significant meaning to the Marcy Randolph case. He immediately logged onto the Internet and to the amazement of the documentary producers found an area just northwest of the Sedona Airport known as Bear Circle. He was ecstatic, feeling that N2700Q had crashed in that area or was on that course out of Sedona. Robinson's GPS coordinate was 1 ½ miles from where the plane was found – in an area known as Bear Forest.

What about the number 121? This may fall into the arena of coincidence, but psychics will tell you they do not believe in coincidence. During his visit to Arizona Robinson met with Baldwin and asked him to dowse a compass direction. He did not mention any numbers or directions. Baldwin got the number 121. This appeared to be significant because a 121 degree heading out of Sedona Airport leads to Munds Park, one of the area's Marcy Randolph planned on flying over.

As previously noted, psychic information is accurate. Where searches often get tripped up is in the interpretation of that information. N2700Q crashed northwest of Sedona, not northeast. Using a 360 degree compass, the bearing from the airport to the crash site was Nearly 330 degrees, close to due north. It appeared that the number 121 was an interesting and potentially valuable clue that just didn't pan out.

After the case was officially closed one of the psychics did a bit of out of the box thinking. Using the precise coordinates of the crash site, Google Earth and a 360 degree compass he discovered that the Sedona Airport is 121 degrees southeast of the crash site.

"If you have men who will exclude any of God's creatures from the shelter of compassion and pity, you will have men who will deal likewise with their fellow men."

~St. Francis of Assisi

CHAPTER FOUR: MARK (TED) STOVER

FROM: KELLY

TO: (FIND ME)

SENT: Tuesday, September 07, 2010 10.44 a.m.

SUBJECT: New Assignment

RESPONSE DUE SEPTEMBER 14TH, 2010 – Please Don't Be Late

SCROLL DOWN FOR DETAILS

MARK STOVER (TED)

DOB: 03/18/1952

POB: Seattle, Washington

TOB: Estimated at 6 p.m.

When someone shoots at your investigating team, there's a good chance you're on to something and in this case that something was the probably location of Mark Stover's body as pinpointed by Find Me psychics. The report filed by AZ-STAR leader Kristi Smith illustrates the dangers Find Me and its search and rescue sister group can encounter.

"(GPS location). Salvage Yard. At approximately 2:21:17 we

were approaching the salvage yard from the North moving in a Southerly direction, intending on searching around the structures and boats, when shots were fired from a High powered handgun originating from SE of us. Three shots were fired in fairly quick succession then three more sporadically fired over the next three minutes. The last shot was fired at approximately 2:24:04 as we went behind the large boat at the Salvage Yard. We were not able to properly search around this salvage yard due to this."

* * *

The Mark Stover case proved equally satisfying and frustrating for the Find Me team. Several psychics identified a specific location for his body, yet circumstances prevented recovery. A suspect was apprehended, arrested, tried and convicted for the crime, yet Mark Stover's body has never been found. Snyder says, "We had what we consider two major hits on the Mark Stover case. One, the gunfire aimed at our search teams seems to be enough confirmation that we have located a specific area where his body was dumped or at least where the body has been carried by tides and currents. Two, a large number of the psychics predicted that the person who was eventually caught, arrested and tried and convicted in court was the murderer – long before he was caught."

The Dog Whisperer

Mark Stover opened the back door to his Anacortes home in far northwest Washington State at 6:30 a.m. Oct. 28, 2009. At his side was Dingo, a beautiful Belgium Malinois he trained for protection. Dingo was a great dog, but could do nothing when a shot from a .22 caliber hand gun smashed into his face. Dingo survived the shooting, but Mark did not survive the shots that followed.

When the authorities searched the house they found lots of blood and plenty of evidence that more blood had been cleaned up with bleach. Mark's body was not found. Land and water searches were conducted by the Skagit County Sheriff's Office and the Skagit Dive Rescue team. Eventually, Find Me was called to assist in the case. Again, due to the late date of the call this was probably a case of, "We've tried everything else, we may as well call in the psychics."

A BUSINESS BUILT FROM THE DOGS; A MARRIAGE GONE TO THE DOGS

In the 1990s Mark (57) married somewhat late in life to Linda Opdycke (45), the daughter of Wallace (Wally) Opdycke, a well-known co-founder of one of Washington's biggest wineries. He had a reputation for being a tough guy in more areas than wine making. He had many business interests. To say that Linda Opdycke was the daughter of wealth and power would be an understatement.

The Stovers founded Island Dog Adventures on an island owned by her family. They worked hard and prospered, offering a variety of services including training, behavioral modification, weight-loss programs, pedicures and manicures. The dogs were allowed free run throughout the island. It should have been an idyllic location for all the two-legged and four-legged inhabitants.

Mark had a special talent and a special philosophy for working with dogs, even challenging animals who were on the verge of being put down. He said he understood dog psychology and the pack mentality. In training sessions he became the alpha male and eventually ruled the pack or the individual animal under his care. He wore dark glasses so that the animals, and people, could not "read" him through his eyes and therefore anticipate his moves.

In the best possible sense their business "went to the dogs" and Mark soon was known as the Seattle "Dog Trainer to the Stars." His client list was impressive and included Eddie Vedder of Pearl Jam and former bassist for Nirvana Krist Novoselic, Starbucks chairman Howard Schultz, Seattle Mariners outfielder Ichiro Suzuki, singer Nancy Wilson, filmmaker Cameron Crowe, and the seventies rock group Hart. Mark was liked and respected by the people in the area and was an asset to his community. Uncontrollable dogs in his care became well-mannered and obedient pets who could run in the sun, play and enhance the lives of their owners instead of becoming a sad memory of an animal given away or put down. After visiting the island, one of his famous clients told a national magazine, "People should have it so good."

The dogs did have it good, but the humans faced challenges they could not overcome. Mark and his wife struggled personally through 2005-2006 and finally agreed to go their separate ways in 2007. The divorce granted Opdycke $175,000 for her share of the business, the family SUV and their horse trailer. He got the Porsche and BMW. He refused to hire a lawyer saying that he didn't require those services for dealing with someone he had loved for so long. Washington State was buying the island, so he agreed to move the business to another location.

Things went further downhill from that point.

In April, 2008 Opdycke had a protection order (restraining order) issued against her former husband. She claimed that he was stalking her. He had come to her new home, hid in the bushes and had pointed a gun at her, she said. She also said a neighbor caught him sneaking around the house and going through Opdyke's garbage. Mark was arrested over the incident.

Opdycke also said he always carried a gun and when he cancelled her health insurance he scrawled across the document, "Next time do not call the cops on the guy that controls your healthcare."

Perhaps he slipped even further. Acting on an anonymous tip, a sheriff's deputy stopped Mark and searched for drugs, finding a small amount of marijuana. Mark's friends were steadfast in their belief that he did not use drugs. He was, after all, a certified expert witness in court cases involving behavior of dogs. One whiff of marijuana and you can kiss your reputation in law enforcement and that part of your business goodbye.

Even the Sheriff's Office found the incident puzzling, saying at the time that there were some indications that he was set up. Whether he was set up and whether the incident was related to the murder is unknown – just another mystery to add to the tragedy.

LITTLE BIG MAN

People who saw the movie *Little Big Man* starring Dustin Hoffman watched the story of a white man who became a fierce Sioux warrior under the great leader Crazy Horse. He was a hero. In real life, Little Big Man was a coward and a traitor to his people and his leader. When the soldiers at Ft. Robinson bayonetted Crazy Horse it was Little Big Man who held him down for the killing.

Many of us have "little big men" enter our lives. Linda Opdycke was one. Michael Oakes entered her life claiming to be a body guard. At age 41 Oakes was closer to her age than her previous husband. He was a little man with big ambitions. He became romantically involved with Opdycke, leaped on her coattails and rode them as far as possible – a long walk down a short pier as it turned out.

Oakes was arrested Friday November 14, 2009 for the murder of Mark Stover. On Friday, October 22, 2010 he heard the words, "We the jury find the defendant Michael Glenn Oakes guilty of the crime of murder in the first degree premeditated as charged." His punishment would be 20 – 26 years in prison, a quarter of a century wondering "how dumb could I have been?"

Find My psychics had reported some interesting facts about the case.

Find Me psychic Pam Bedgar reported that the suspect's name started "...with an M like Mike or Michael."

Michele Nappi reported earlier that the suspect would be named Michael.

Dwayne Brock, Patti Rogel, Isabella Johnson were among the members who identified Michael Oakes as the shooter.

HOW NOT TO COMMIT MURDER

Committing murder is easy. But, as Wyatt proved to Curley Bill, Murder Inc. proved to Dutch Schultz, and 77 bullets of varying calibers proved to Bonnie and Clyde, *getting away* with murder is an entirely different matter. Michael Oakes' actions provide a step-by-step guide for the would-be chased, caught and convicted murderer.

Step #1. Come to the scene of the crime scene with a proper weapon and the ability to use that weapon. Some people think a .22 caliber hand gun is little more than a "pop gun" unable to cause serious harm. Nothing could be further from the truth. In fact, .22 caliber pistols are often the preferred weapon for the professional assassin. They are relatively quiet, especially when short-loaded with a less than full charge of powder—as quiet as a silencer. And a couple of small bullets tumbling around the insides of a human torso can create an enormous amount of damage.

Oakes possessed a .22 caliber hand gun. How do we know? The police found it.

Step #2. Come prepared to deal with the body. Think back to *The Sopranos*. Necessary tools of the trade often included a saw or bolt cutter to render the body into manageable sections, plastic bags for easy transportation of body parts, and a bottle or two of bleach to remove blood stains.

Oakes must have arrived prepared to deal with the body because the floor of Mark's house was covered in blood and bleach. He bought bolt cutters, but he kept the receipt and the police found it. He also bought knee pads, apparently as safety/comfort equipment for heavy-duty work on the floor. The police also found a receipt for this unusual element of what appeared to be a murder kit. Preparation should include the ability to properly use the tools for cleaning up the crime, knowledge Oakes obviously lacked.

Many of the psychics picked up on this angle. Here are a few representative samples.

"...there was no struggle, just shooting. An animal feels injured as well. The killer is prepared and hit feels as if he cleans up a bit, not much and changes his clothes...his eyes burning so he could have used bleach to wipe things down..." Isabella Johnson.

"...this is the area where he threw a leg, the leg was cut off from the knee down..." Rebekah Johnson

"...I sense that Mark's body is in pieces and spread out...." Andrea Mackenzie

Step #3. Have a plan to dispose of the body of your victim. This ties in closely with step number two. In a desert or forest the killer would want a shovel and a four-wheel drive vehicle. In town he might employ a backhoe to hide the body at or near a construction site. But Mark lived in an area known for its bays, inlets, waterways and islands. What is the easiest, most convenient and most obvious way to dispose of a body in such an environment?

You guessed it. While examining the ever-growing pile of evidence against Oakes, the authorities found a Walmart security video showing Oakes buying one-pound ankle weights and anchor rope.

The day of the killing Oakes parked a quarter mile from Mark's house behind the Summit Park Grange. Keeping such visual evidence from the scene of the crime sounds like a good idea and it is in the hands of a capable criminal. As you will read, the word "capable" do not accurately reflect the thinking behind the actions of Michael

Glenn Oakes.

Step #4. Disguise yourself. Should a killer be seen, he should make sure that he cannot be identified by the sighting. If there's a chance you'll be seen, a disguise is an essential element of the successful murder. The Walmart security video also showed Oakes purchasing a camouflage sweat suit.

Step #5. Time the crime. A killer does not want to be seen arriving at, committing or escaping from the scene of the crime. The event should be timed to prevent or to at least diminish such exposure. Oakes must have forgotten his watch that day. As he busied himself pouring bleach and wiping up a massive blood spill, he heard voices. Mark's employees who had a firmer grasp on the concept of time showed up for work on schedule. Oakes bailed out with the cover up uncovered.

Step #6. Dispose of the body. St. Francis of Assisi said, "Not to hurt our humble brethren [the animals] is our first duty to them, but to stop there is not enough. We have a higher mission: to be of service to them whenever they require it." In an act of cruelty in direct opposition to the teachings of St. Francis, Oakes tossed the still-breathing Dingo over the fence, leaving the loyal animal to die alone and in great pain. Getting rid of a human body proved to be a greater challenge, but this is the one thing the killer got right and the reason Find Me and later AZSTAR were eventually brought into the case.

Remember Oakes' "carefully hidden" car a quarter mile from the crime scene? It really wasn't all that hidden. Oakes placed the body in Mark's station wagon and drove it to his car for a transfer. A woman living next door saw him transferring something from one car (Mark's) to another (his). She noticed that clear plastic sheeting had been stretched from one vehicle to another, obscuring her view of what was happening. The activity seemed suspicious so she wrote down the license plate numbers of each car. Oakes drove away leaving

Mark's car.

Many of the psychics reported that Mark's body had been dumped in one of the nearby waterways.

"…I feel the body was kept at a pier/boathouse for short period and the moved to dump in water…" Michele Nappi

"…In river or lake there are lots of weeping willows…" Wendy Berkahn

"…in deep water…" Alex Stark

"…I feel Mark's body has been dumped into a canal or bay connected to the ocean…" Rich Bunch

"…a river, drops downwards/moves downwards – a jagged pathway...dumped in a river/water…" Daz Smith.

"…He is near a body of water and wash ashore…" Tammy Carpenter

"…body weighted and in water…" Dan Baldwin

"…drove the boat out a ways and dumped his body in the water. It looks like it may be lodged among some debris like old logs, wood fragments and garbage debris…" Rose Mancuso

"…he was moved over water to the (GPS) location above. Most likely be ferry or boat…" Dennis Hanna

"…held under water by wire/chains wrapped around garbage bag of dismembered body…" Peggy Rometo

"…I'm seeing some water. It looks round, but larger than a pond, like a lake…" Wendy Ishie-Katen

"…body is in water (Kiket Bay) just north of Kiket Island…" Dwayne Brock

It is important to note that the GPS coordinates were included in the psychics' reports. The rather general descriptions just cited were accompanied by extremely accurate target locations.

Step #7. Don't incriminate yourself. The more a criminal talks the more evidence he provides. According to court documents, Oakes met with his wife just after the killing.

He told her that a big and dangerous "mission" had gone "bad." He said that if the police saw what was inside his car he would go to prison for life. He seemed to have been driven by guilt, a need for punishment, or just plain stupidity.

When the police scrolled through his computer's history, they found a "how to dismember a body" site. The police got a search warrant for the computer and its contents, but forgot to include the house in which the computer was stored in their paperwork. The "how to…" never made it into evidence. Although there are always lapses in judgment in any investigation, Oakes was leaving enough incriminating clues that the bumbling teams from Reno 911, Police Squad, and even the Keystone Kops could track his movements.

Step #8. Have a simple and credible alibi. This is where Oakes in the "how not to" category really shines. Having botched the cover up, he began implementing his futile attempts at establishing an alibi.

First there's that visit to his wife, the one where he mentioned the mission "gone bad." She lived an hour and a half away which means he was not at the scene of the crime 90 minutes after it occurred. It proves nothing of value. This is the type of "alibi" prosecuting attorneys dream of.

He headed back to Anacortes and somewhere along the way disposed of the body. He drove to the Swinomish Indian Reservation's Northern Lights Casino. His apparent purpose was to have the car recorded on the casino's security cameras so that it would appear the owner was inside enjoying the area's gaming experience.

Oakes disappears for a few hours, returned to the casino with Mark's station wagon, parked and left it. Police later found a blood stain on the vehicle. Things get even worse from here.

Bye Bye Alibi

Not surprisingly, the Skagit County Sheriff's Office tracked down Oakes the next day. Anyone watching the crime shows on television has noticed that the guilty party usually plays it cool right until the moment he or she is tripped up by CSI, SVU or NCIS. Oakes began tripping, stumbling and falling all over his alibi the second the authorities arrived.

Saying he needed to get some medicine, he ran to his car and *while the deputies watched* grabbled a white plastic bag and threw it over a nearby embankment. When recovered, the deputies discovered a .22 semi-automatic pistol. The bag smelled like bleach.

A number of psychics reported the use of plastic bags or a plastic tarp in the commission of the crime.

"...he rolls the body up in a tarp or plastic bags that he has brought..." Isabella Johnson

"...it was wrapped up in a tarp..." Rebekah Johnson

"...I saw he was decapitated...put in a plastic bag..." Pam Bedgar Oakes also had possession of a 9mm hand gun. He also had a bullet proof vest, which was used against him in court.

Well, if one alibi doesn't work, maybe another will. He gave up on the "I wasn't at the scene of the crime when it happened because my dog ate my homework" line and moved on. Now he *was* there and he did shoot and kill Mark—in self-defense. It seems that Mark had invited him over for a talk. Oakes wore his bullet-proof vest used in his security training because he believed Mark wanted to kill him.

When he arrived Mark shot him, but the bullet lodged in the vest. Oakes, ever the proficient security trainer, took the weapon and fired, killing Mark. Somehow knowing or suspecting the worse, he had made all those unusual and apparently-incriminating Walmart purchases for self-protection just before the confrontation.

When the police examined the bullet proof vest they couldn't find a bullet or even an indention indicating a hit.

Oakes told the authorities that his plan was to wear the camouflage suit in case he needed to escape Mark and Dingo. If chased, his goal was to dash to a nearby water tower where he would tie the one-pound weights to the anchor rope, toss the rope so he could reach the tower's ladder and make his escape. This line of alleged thinking requires two beliefs: (1) the raging Mark and Dingo giving chase would pause to share a couple of doggie treats to allow Oakes the required time to perform these tasks, and (2) hanging out in the open air from a ladder is a good place to escape from a man carrying a loaded pistol. His alibis had more holes than that ladder.

Apparently, all his plans went sour and he had to kill to protect himself. He decided the best thing to do was to get rid of the body. He dumped Mark's remains into the sea from an old dock behind the casino.

A lot of questions surround this case.

Oakes did a lot of running around right after the killing. Did he have a co-conspirator?

Was someone else involved directly in the killing?

What was the reason for the possible "set up" involving marijuana?

Was the "set up" part of the plan?

How did he get from the casino to Mark's car some three miles back at the grange building? Was there an accomplice who drove him? Did he hitchhike? Walk?

Did someone pay or threaten him to commit the crime?

What was he doing during all those missing hours?

And most important, where is Mark Stover's body?

As a family member told the Seattle Times, "...we won't have full closure until he is found."

At the Scene of the Crime

Preparation for the trial sapped most of the Skagit County Sheriff's Office's time and personnel which left very little time to search for Mark's body. That's understandable. They had a case that was about as solid as it gets and they naturally focused their energies on "dotting every "I" and crossing every "T" to insure a conviction. Leigh Herron, a well-respected private investigator known for her skill level and due diligence was hired to follow up on finding Mark's body. She called Snyder. Would Find Me be interested in taking on the case of Mark Stover?

Snyder followed the proper and well-established protocol with local law enforcement and then sent the case to the members of Find Me. The case brought with it a sense of urgency. Once a body is buried in the earth or hidden in some structure, it stays in place. Rare exceptions exist, of course. Earthquakes, floods, landslides, building demolitions and so on can move a hidden body, but, again, these are exceptions. Once a body is placed in a body of water the creatures living there begin their usual destructive work. Of greater concern is that a body in water is likely to be moved by rising and lowering tides, swift currents or even the motion of watercraft. Such movement may begin the moment the body is dropped into the water. This is one reason four psychics can have four different locations for a missing person with each reading accurate. The body is up river, mid river, down river or in the bay or ocean fed by the river because it is in motion at the different times of each reading. Psychic detectives often face this challenge, especially when tracking an individual on the move who may cover hundreds of miles during the allotted time for the psychics to conduct their research.

Some of the psychics believed that three conspirators were involved: Oakes, another male and a female with Oakes being the shooter, the theory being that all three were involved in planning the killing and would share any profits from the venture.

Most of the psychics' hits (body location) were within a five mile area. GPS coordinates and physical descriptions pinpointed specific areas for search. It should be noted again that such variances in specifics are natural and to be expected. Most psychics will tell you that the information coming in is always correct. Errors that creep into an investigation are due solely to the psychic's interpretation of that information. Once all the reports were in and the information coordinated, Find Me and AZSTAR made arrangements to fly to Anacortes for an on-the-scene investigation. Kristi Smith, AZSTAR founder and a dog handler in the same league as Mark (or better) brought her dog Kiki. Other handlers in the group brought their dogs. Dog handlers were searching for a missing dog trainer – what irony.

Find Me psychics pinpointed 23 possible sites for Mark's body. Fortunately for the search team, many of them were within a few hundred feet of each other—within the same search grid. Each site was thoroughly investigated and the information recorded for later analysis, compilation and submission to the proper authorities.

One of those sites was on Kikit Island, the location where Mark and Opdycke had lived. Kiki alerted (showed interest) in a few locations. Protocol states that at least one other dog, if available, should verify such an alert. One of the other dogs showed definite interest in the same sites, confirming the original alert. Something definitely happened on the northwest corner of the island near a broken down boat launch. Remember that Oakes had stated he dumped Mark's body from a rundown boat launch, albeit at another location.

The double alerts were enough to encourage the teams to return the following day to rent a boat and continue the search on water. Contrary to popular fiction, well-trained dogs can easily follow a scent across open water.

The small watercraft was just large enough for the boat handler, investigator Herron's brother, a dog handler and a dog. Each dog had a separate shift to see if he or she alerted at the same locations. Both dogs alerted at the same location and the information was rapidly given to the Skagit County Sheriff's Office.

What followed is an all too common example of why talented psychics can become frustrated psychics. One would expect the sheriff's office to send out a dive team to investigate the site. After all: (1) numerous psychics hit on that specific location, (2) the island was important to the victim and a possible suspect or suspects, and (3) two extremely well-trained search dogs with proven track records alerted at the same location. Although dive teams were available—they had participated in earlier and fruitless searches—they weren't called.

Why?

The prosecutor in the case dispatched a boat with a local cadaver dog and the animal failed to alert at the designated sites. End of story. There were no more searches, no dive team was called, no camera was sent below for a look. The locations the Find Me AZSTAR teams provided were precise and the resources were available. Why the sheriff's office decided to halt its efforts is a mystery.

The Skagit County Sheriff's Office may have given up on the location, but Find Me and AZSTAR remained on the case. A week later Smith and Kiki returned. This time they brought a professional diver who is part of their team. The depth of water at that location was deeper than expected, but a thorough search was conducted. Mark's body was not found.

As this chapter is being written, Mark's body is still missing. But there is hope. Oakes is serving time, a lot of time. Certainly much of it will be spent considering his situation and the varying futures he faces. If, as some members of Find Me believe, he has partners, it is in their interest to see him come to harm. The sheriff's office and the prosecutor are probably applying pressure and maybe offering a deal if he will talk.

That's a terrible risk for any co-conspirators.

Terrible crimes occur in prison and you would be amazed at how clever prisoners are at crafting deadly weapons out of the most innocuous objects. Half a razor blade inserted into the handle of a toothbrush becomes a deadly knife. If no blade is available, the tip of the toothbrush can be ground and smoothed down to a sharp point to be used as a shiv. A piece of broken window glass in the right hands becomes a sword. And " accidents" happen all the time.

Oakes' safety can only be somewhat guaranteed by placing him in protective custody or solitary confinement. And even if none of these worst-case scenarios play out he still faces a quarter century behind bars. His motivation to talk increases with every breath he takes.

Unless asked, the psychics and the dog teams are out of the picture. The team has done its job and has done it well. The rest is up to the organizations with legal authority and power. Find Me and AZ-STAR have given law enforcement "the ball." It is now up to those groups to run with it.

"Humor is one of God's most marvelous gifts.
Humor gives us smiles, laughter, and gaiety.
Humor reveals the roses and hides the thorns."

~Sen. Sam Ervin

CHAPTER FIVE: WILLIE JIGBA

FROM: KELLY

TO: (FIND ME LIST)

SENT: Monday, January 24, 2011 6:23 p.m.

SUBJECT: MISSING ASU STUDENT

SPECIAL REQUEST MEMBERS.

(Newspaper article link)

I searched yesterday for six hours, but the windy conditions ruined our search efforts. I will be searching again on Wednesday morning with our canine group. Please respond with your location information no later than tomorrow January 25th. Thanks

WILLIE JIGBA

DOB: 12/07/1986

POB: L.A. California

Left a party at 615 E. Weber Dr. Tempe, AZ at 3:00 a.m. headed to his apartment which is approximately 2 miles away on foot. He has not been seen since.

Twenty-four year old, six foot tall Willie Jigba had the gift of humor so praised by Sam Ervin. Although not an Arizona State University student, he lived close to ASU and was friends with many students. One of those friends, Gaby Assour, said, "He was the one who always had everyone laughing." His roommate, Reggie Halstrom said, He was the nicest guy you'd ever meet" and recalled his carefree spirit. McKenzie Coates, another student, called Willie a mediator because when problems flared "he was always the first person to give you ten reasons why you should be friends."

Jigba came to Arizona from California. He worked at a local restaurant, saving his money so he could attend nearby Mesa Community College the following year.

The laughter died sometime after 3:00 or 3:30 a.m. January 15.

A Bridge to Nowhere

The party that night was great. Willie was with a lot of his friends and his joy must have been expressed on his well-known "big crooked smile." If not the life of the party, Willie could be counted on to put some life into a party. Naturally, the drinks flowed and some later said that their friend may have allowed too much to flow his way. Although Tempe is a university town used to the ways of students, there are limits, especially on noise during the early hours of the morning. Police officers were called and the party came to an end. Willie's cell phone had died and he couldn't call for someone to pick him up. No one at the party was willing to drive him back, so Willie decided to walk the two and a half miles to his apartment – an easy walk for a young man in good condition even if a bit inebriated.

As he walked away, those who saw him were the last to see Willie Jigba alive.

The logical route to his residence would be to walk down Curry Street to Scottsdale Road, a busy main drag any time of the day or night, and turn south. This course would take him to one of the bridges over the man-made Tempe Town Lake. Frommers travel guide calls the lake "perhaps the most unusual park in the Phoenix metro area." The lake was created in 1999 by damming the Salt River, which runs east-west through Phoenix and much of the Valley of the Sun. It is two-miles long and features parks and bike paths on the north and south shores. Small boats and kayaks dot the surface during the day time hours. During that January week the water temperature was between 40 and 45 degrees.

Tempe Town Lake is considered a great place to enjoy nature, to study, play or to just relax and watch people having a good time. For anyone who falls in and is injured or impaired, it is a deadly environment, especially when the water temperature can quickly induce hypothermia.

Willie never returned to his apartment. The hope of his friends was that he was sleeping it off somewhere safe. But there were concerns. He was supposed to begin a new job at 10 a.m. that morning. He normally checked in with his friends, but Assour assumed that he had simply forgotten to call. Later, as it became clear that no one had heard from the usually-reliable young man, friends began making calls and even retracing his likely track from the party to his apartment. They found no sign of their friend.

A former co-worker, Jenn Brown, said, "He wouldn't just get up and skip town like this. Everybody loves Willie. He wouldn't just leave and do that to his family."

That Sunday his family reported him missing to the Tempe Police Department.

Unfortunately protocol meant they couldn't begin an immediate search for the missing young man. Willie was an adult free to come and go as he pleased with or without notifying anyone. There was no indication of foul play, a suicide note, an indication that he was about to harm someone or that there was anything out of the ordinary – other than the disappearance. He had money, friends, was mobile and could be simply be off on a lark. Hindsight is 20/20, but even knowing what is known now it is easy to understand the position taken by the department at the time.

Willie's friends began searching, passing out flyers, knocking on doors and even set up a missing person Facebook page. Willie's father, Emmanuel Jigba, knew his son and his son's behavior. He arrived three days after the disappearance to help with the search.

FIND ME'S SPECIAL REQUEST GROUP GETS THE CALL

Several people involved in the search knew about AZ STAR and Kristi Smith was soon contacted. While organizing AZSTAR's teams she called Snyder to get things rolling on the Find Me side.

Find Me had recently instituted a Special Request Group. These are volunteers who have agreed to stand ready for special emergency alerts that required a response significantly faster than the normal procedure. Generally the response is requested within 24 hours of getting the call.

While the psychics were engaging their various skills, Kristi and her canine, Kiki, checked the location of the party. Kiki picked up a scent and took Kristi along a path that was consistent with the one Willie would have most likely taken to get back to his apartment. That course took them to Tempe Town Lake.

The Find Me Special Request Group was busy, too. For example, one member immediately had a vision of "the big picture," which she began to break down into its various elements. She believed Willie had fallen off something into the water and that he may have hit his head on something and drowned.

Baldwin, who lives in the Mesa not too far from the lake, used his pendulum and doused a location east of the bridge on Mill St., one of two crossing the lake. The body was underwater near one of the walk paths. He provided GPS co-ordinates as required by the group's protocols. The other members of the response team acted just as quickly.

With the psychic information in hand, searches of Tempe Town Lake began on January 23, 2011. Kristi and Kiki were joined by other members of the group and their dogs.

This was a search requiring travel over water. Unfortunately, the only craft AZSTAR had available was an eight-foot by four ½ foot raft purchased for another mission some years earlier. It was unstable and hardly the best platform for such work, but since the only other option was to search a lake without actually going on the lake, the raft had to do. Thoroughness is a hallmark of Find Me and AZSTAR procedures and sometimes risks are involved.

Kristi and Kiki and Snyder took the first cruise around the lake, taking a serpentine route as the approached the bridge to make sure the current had not carried the body downstream and out of the primary search area.

Kiki gave an indication that to Kristi suggested she was interested in a particular area. The team circled the area eight times to make sure that the interest was genuine. After returning to shore, another team was given the raft and told to search the target area. It is protocol for the first team NOT to tell the follow up team where interest has been shown to prevent any possible contamination of the final report. The results of their search indicated the same location. The third team followed the same procedure with the same result. Three teams had independently indicated a location within a few feet of each other. Wind and choppy waters prevented additional searching that day.

Throughout this process, Emmanuel Jigba watched from the dock hoping and praying that his son was still alive – somewhere. He said, "I just want to find him and if he is dead I can bring him home and bury him. I don't want to never know where my son is. I need to know where he is. If he is dead I need to know that."

A CLEAR VISION IN MURKY WATERS

Kristi believed that the group should conduct one more search. She wanted indisputable evidence that *someone* was in the lake at that location. The search began on January 25 with Kristi and Kiki. Again, the search dogs showed interest in the same area. It was time to contact the authorities.

The Tempe Fire Department Dive Team was notified and dive master Chuck Herman didn't waste a second. His entire team showed up at 1:30 p.m. to begin what is known as a "fan search" of the lake. This is a technique in which divers start from a specific location and then fan out in all directions to cover the entire search area. It is a tedious, but very thorough process and has proven highly effective. Their search efforts were hampered by terrible conditions. The cold water was murky with visibility limited to about 18 inches. Under such conditions, searchers have to feel their way around to compensate for the lack of vision.

The search was negative as was a second search the following day. This would have been the inevitable "it," the end of the search for the dive team and there was little else to do. The psychics had pinpointed a specific location and multiple and well-trained dog teams had independently backed them up.

This should give you an idea of the frustration often felt my many of the psychics. When the ones who are "on" on a given day indicate a location they *know* the missing person is there. Yet they are constrained and prevented from finding that person by elements or forces out of their control, such as distance, financial considerations, private property rights, police procedures and other legitimate reasons.

Fortunately, Chuck Herman was willing to follow his own intuition. He, too believed Willie was in the lake and at the designated location. The feeling was so strong that he couldn't sleep. That "nagging at the back of the head" psychics are so familiar with would not give him peace. At about 9:30 the morning of the 27th he drove back to the lake for another look. After a few minutes, when his eyes adjusted to the light and the sun beaming off the waves, he saw a body. He contacted the dive team and within half an hour the body was on shore. The physical description and the clothing matched those of Willie Jigba. According to police procedures the medical examiner was called to the scene to examine the body. No evidence of foul play was indicated.

Seven psychics stated that Willie was in the Tempe Town Lake. Three were close to where he was eventually found and at least three were within less than a mile of where he was located. Our hits included (1) he was deceased, (2) that he was in the water, (3) that he was in Tempe Town Lake, and most importantly (4) multiple psychics pinpointed locations only a few feet from where he was found.

Willie Jigba was found within 30 feet of where Find Me psychics had placed him and precisely where the AZSTAR scent dogs had alerted. As Snyder later noted in an e-mail to Find Me, "This is a perfect example of what we can do… it also proved to the Tempe Police and Tempe Fire Dept. that psychics, retired law enforcement, and canine SAR can work together for a common cause."

The ending to this case, as with so many, cannot be said to be happy in the traditional sense. But the combined efforts of dedicated individuals and organizations were able to bring closure to family and friends. Emmanuel Jigba was able to take his son home.

"What prodigious power a large body of men can put forth when they all work at the same task...."

~William Graham Sumner

Chapter Six: Jack Culolias

From: Kelly Snyder

To: Find Me

Sent: December 10, 2013

Subject: Jack Culolias

Last seen at Cadillac Ranch in Tempe Town Marketplace, 2000 E. Rio Salado Parkway, Tempe, AZ on December 1st 2012 and has not been seen since. I need your information ASAP. We will start our search with the dogs as soon as we have your information.
Kelly

(From azcentral.com) "Search-and-rescue teams found a body Sunday morning floating in the water north of Tempe Marketplace that Tempe police said could be an Arizona State University student who disappeared two weeks ago… Arizona Search Track and Rescue and Find Me, two groups not affiliated with the Tempe Police Department found the body at about 10:20 a.m.…"

The Culolias case proves the effectiveness and the efficiency of working with dedicated psychics partnered with well-trained search-and-rescue teams. Neither group claims a 100 percent success rate, yet when all the elements come together, when all the tumblers click into place, the partnership works incredibly well in solving crimes, finding missing persons, and bringing closure to grieving families.

Regardless of the hard work and diligent efforts of the Tempe Police Department, Maricopa County Sheriff's Office rescue team and lake patrol, ASU detectives, K-9 units, ground-search units, and helicopters from the Phoenix and Mesa police departments, *Jack Culolias remained missing until Find Me and AZSTAR were called in.*

* * *

Jack Culolias was considered something of a jokester by his friends. He was an energetic extrovert. He was close to his father, George, and his twin, Alex, and his other brother Nick. George Culolias died of lung cancer before Jack left for ASU and according to friends, Jack took his father's passing hard and apparently saw the move to college as something of an escape from his sadness or at least a diversion from it. Perhaps personal sadness was a prime motivating emotion behind his decision to pledge Sigma Alpha Epsilon fraternity.

Jack disappeared about 11 p.m. Nov. 30 after he left the Cadillac Ranch at Tempe Marketplace. The news media reported that he had been escorted out by security due to inebriation which occurred at a fraternity event that evening.

No one saw him again until his body was recovered from the nearby Tempe Town Lake. When Culolias didn't return to school, his fraternity brothers contacted his step-mother, Renae Culolias, who contacted the ASU authorities and reported her son missing on Dec. 2nd. The official search began on Dec. 4th and lasted through Dec. 7th. Culolias had been wearing jeans, a black shirt, and red tennis shoes. Jack was so proud of his red shoes that he wore them all the time, even to formal events.

Renae accompanied by Grace, his biological mother, came in from California and demanded that the Tempe police begin an investigation. The ASU Police were reacting to the situation as if it was a fraternity prank at first. That attitude changed Dec. 4th when it was decided that the incident was clearly something beyond a prank or a pledge initiation and was a Tempe Police Department matter.

Family and friends began searching the area and that afternoon Grace called the ASU police to tell them that she had located one of Jack's red shoes on the lakeside just north of Tempe Marketplace. Later, DNA testing proved it to be one of Jack's shoes or at least one that he had worn. The intense search mentioned earlier in this chapter began, but with no results.

The Psychics Work – Underwater

Renae Culolias contacted Find Me on Wednesday, Dec. 12th and asked for help from the psychics. Snyder sent out the standard e-mail to the 120 psychics in the group at that time. Approximately 60 responded. Psychics can get extraordinarily accurate hits when researching a case. Unlike events portrayed in the movies and on television, sometimes they draw a blank. Of those reporting, 35 said that Jack was deceased and that Jack was located in Tempe Town Lake near Tempe Marketplace. The information was limited to just a generic area beneath the nearby bridge of the 202 and the 101 highways.

Later, as more reports came in, the possible location of Jack's body was narrowed to a smaller area of the lake. For example, seven psychics reported GPS coordinates that were within a hundred yards of where his body was found. The closest were Kristine Pomeroy, Dave Campbell, Patricia Monna, Dwayne Brock, and Dan Baldwin.

Psychic Dwayne Brock reported that he had been driving across the Mill Avenue bridge over Tempe Town Lake the evening Jack disappeared. "I got sick as a dog. I mean all of a sudden, I just felt like I was drowning. I couldn't breathe and I was being smothered." Brock says he communicated with Jack's spirit. "He was telling me that he was in the water and that he wanted to go home."

Most of the psychics reported Jack in the lake.

"...I feel the victim is in water, not far from the area where he was last seen...." Laura Traplin.

"...I feel like Jack's death is due to an accidental drowning in the lake that is next to the mall... I believe his body will be found if the check the northeast part of the river..." Patricia Monna.

"...On the lake. He is in the water... I see lots of rocks and debris around him. I know he is in the river (Tempe Town Lake)...." Dave Campbell.

"...in the water, half way between north side of the canal and center. I do see his spirit and do not feel he is alive..." Wendy Ishie-Katen.

"...Deceased Body in creek like area... trees, brush around, yet not too far from cement structures..." Kristine Pomeroy

"I feel there is a bend to the right in the flow of the landscape and he is on the left of this partially covered in what looks like leafy dried and dead material..." Wendy Berkahn

TEAMWORK TURNS THE INVESTIGATIVE TIDE

A standard AZSTAR search was scheduled and a number of Find Me members volunteered as ground pounders. The two search groups arrived Saturday morning before dawn to prepare for the day's search. A bright, interior lighted billboard rose above the nearby interstate. One of the flashing ads was a missing persons poster of Jack Culolias.

It was as if the young student was watching over the efforts of his own recovery. Search areas included an industrial dump site just south of the lake and due ease of a Tempe Marketplace parking lot. Other sites focused on the edge of the lake a few yards away. The lakeshore was extremely overgrown with thick grass, shrubs and trees and was also littered with an enormous amount of trash – an extremely challenging couple of areas for humans and dogs. The areas were separated by a tall and steep incline leading from the dump site/marketplace area down to the lake. Previous search efforts came across what could have been slide marks of someone slipping down this dangerous incline. Find Me members Snyder, Baldwin, Kelly Townsend and Julia D'Alphonso were also assisting in the search with AZ STAR whose search dogs alerted on a specific area at the southeastern end of the lake. One of the dogs, Jetson, almost pulled his handler into the lake. "He was pulling with such force that I was gearing myself up to jump into the cold water to help pull her out if he dragged her in. Fortunately, that wasn't necessary," Baldwin said.

Snyder notified the Tempe Police Department that the two groups were going to be conducting a water search with a boat the following day. Three of the dogs alerted on the shoreline, but the search team leaders wanted to put the dogs in the boat to see if they could determine a more specific site.

Jack's story provides a good example of the "many pieces of the puzzle" approach taken by Find Me. Re-read the psychics' clues a few paragraphs back. Individually, they are helpful, but hardly enough alone to pinpoint the location of a body. Now, consider the totality of those reports compared to the events that followed. Jack's body was found in a narrow, creek-like area on the eastern edge of Tempe Town Lake. The body surfaced next to an area of dried, weedy growth and directly under a large concrete highway overpass. Remember, too, that the psychics filed GPS coordinates to back up their findings, so these locations were by no means lucky guesses.

The following day Find Me and AZSTAR went to the same area where the dogs had alerted. Prior to the search, Snyder asked the search commander for that day, Thomas K. Wind, if they could conduct one more search of the area with one of their dogs. The dog, Jetson was Terrie Davies dog. Kathleen, one of the AZSTAR members, went along. Within five minutes they had a Code F-3, which indicates that a body has been located in the search area. Snyder went immediately to the scene. The searchers felt strongly that the body was Jack, but, of course, at that time the determination was not possible.

However, in short order, the body was positively identified as Jack Culolias.

Kristi Smith, founder and leader of AZSTAR, and Snyder stated to the media their wish that the authorities in these cases would contact their groups from the initial moment of the investigation. This is especially true of the psychics who time and again have proven the value of psychic research teamed with a SAR teams. Snyder says, "My goal is to prove to not only the public and the police, but to all of humanity that this stuff really does work."

It doesn't take any stretch of the imagination to believe the Culolias family would agree.

* * *

As this book neared its final stages Snyder received the following note from Renae Culolias:

Kelly,

I just wanted to thank you for all of your help and support in finding Jack Culolias! It is organizations like yours that make a difference in this world. I just can't thank you enough for bring Jack home to us and for not giving up (even though it wasn't the way we wanted him back). If there is ever anything that I or my family can ever do for you, please let us know.

Sincerly,

Renae

"When truth is buried, it grows, it chokes, it gathers such explosive force that on the day it breaks out, it blows everything up with it."

~Emile Zola

Chapter Seven: Deborah Heriford

From: Kelly Snyder

To: Find Me

Sent: Sunday, March 25, 2012 9:45 AM

Subject: New Assignment – Due March 31, 2012

Deborah Heriford

DOB: 05/21/1959

POB: St. Johns, Newfoundland, Canada

TOB: Unknown

Deborah was last seen (confirmed at 3:45 P.M. on March 31st 2011- at 2725 Maroon Bells Ave., Colorado Springs, Colorado (her residence). The Colorado Springs Police have asked for our assistance in locating Deborah.

Thanks,

Kelly

Fire Above and Below

"That fire on the mountain is moving pretty damn fast." Baldwin told Snyder about a fire he had noticed during a break while a search was being organized in Colorado Springs. Several members of Find Me and AZSTAR had traveled to the high country to help the authorities search for a missing woman. Snyder said, "Some of our hits are up in that area. This could be trouble." And it was trouble. The small fire became the largest wildfire in Colorado history and it was just one that would impact the search.

* * *

Deborah Heriford was to most people a pretty typical American middle class working woman. She was 51 years old, 5' 4" tall, weighed about 160 lbs. and had brown hair and brown eyes. She had been married to one man for 32 years. They had three children – Dan, Sarah and Christine or "Chrissy." Deborah worked as a crossing guard for the Discovery Canyon Campus elementary area for Academy School district 20 and she attended the Vista Grande Baptist Church. Deborah was also a woman betrayed by the man she loved.

The suspicion of betrayal leaves a person feeling empty. When those suspicions are confirmed the person is shattered and Deborah Heriford was certainly a shattered woman the spring of 2011. Her husband, Harold "Rob" Heriford, was a lifer in the military – most of his career spent as a police officer. He had served as the head of the military police at Peterson Air Force Base in Colorado Springs. He knew crime, criminals, the criminal mind and a criminal's tricks of the trade. Deborah believed he had been cheating on her for much of the previous year. She also suspected Rob of diverting money and personal holdings for his own use. Tired of the empty, not-knowing feeling, she hired a forensic accountant who confirmed her worst fears.

Deborah and her husband separated in September, 2010 with a final divorce settlement scheduled for May, 2011. Rob had not only hidden more than a million dollars, but was selling and converting property to his name, a process that continued until the day Deborah disappeared – March 31, 2011.

That afternoon she left their house in the 2700 block of Bells Avenue, Colorado Springs, at 3:45 to walk her dog, which was common practice. A neighbor saw her walking down her favorite walking path. Nothing seemed out of the ordinary. Deborah also spoke to her attorney about her pending divorce at 4:00 p.m. That was the last contact anyone who cared about or was concerned about her had with Deborah.

Her dog was located later that day at a strip mall near the area, but Deborah was gone. She had no serious medical condition that would cause concern for a disappearance. When the police were called in they noted that there was no sign of forced entry at the house and there were no signs of foul play in the home or in the immediate neighborhood. The community responded immediately with more than 100 neighbors distributing thousands of missing person flyers and investing their time walking the streets, alleys and nearby parks. "This is a suspicious missing person case. We're investigating it and we're not ruling anything in or out at this point," said police spokesman Sgt. Steve Norbitt.

Where was Rob when his wife disappeared?

He was absent from his job. He also could not or would not account for 16 hours around the time of the disappearance. Another person connected to the case was missing almost the same 16 hours from his/her schedule. It is speculated that this person was involved with Rob in – something.

The case became more intense in May. "We're now investigating this as if it's a homicide," said Detective Derek Graham of the Colorado Police Department. Graham had been working the case since day one. "She didn't show up for work on Friday, totally out of character for her, she had not talked to her sister who she talked to daily, so there were a lot of concerns when we initially got involved that there may be something suspicious," he added. Later, Find Me would encounter challenges in working with Det. Graham – a small firestorm itself.

Rob Heriford lawyered up immediately and refused to cooperate. The person named as a potential co-conspirator was not interviewed as of the date of our search and detective Graham offered no excuse for that except "he will get to it soon." As this chapter is being written his progress has been slow and it appears that he is stumped as to where and what to do in the investigation.

Matters became even more intense for Deborah's children. Sarah filed a restraining order against her father on April 8th stating that she feared for her safety. She also claimed that he was trying to get his hands on items from the home. The family had secured Deborah's belongings in a locked and guarded storage facility. Chrissy also filed a restraining order against Heriford. She said he threatened her in a text message that read, "If you don't give me what I want we are going to have issues."

He was having his own set of ups and downs. The divorce, scheduled for May 24th, was never granted because one of the principles, Deborah, was not present for the hearing. The judge would not allow the final decree. This also meant that Heriford had to continue making his alimony payments because his wife was not legally dead. Emotionally, he seemed to have moved on. He and his girlfriend, Karen Vindelov, had planned on getting married as soon as the divorce was final. Obviously, that could never happen. Again, legally his wife had not been declared dead. Regardless of the law, he and Karen held a pseudo-wedding ceremony. Although not legal, they did exchange vows.

During the summer, the police impounded his car and Karen's car. Chrissy hired a private investigator in September. "Things have been quiet and it's time to get this investigation going again," she said.

Chrissy Finds Find Me

Chrissy contacted Find Me on March 08, 2012. She wrote, "…I am begging you to help me. I know you don't talk with family members, but I am willing to give you any/all details that might help you to help the police with her case… whatever you need… please." They psychics were soon to join the search.

As is customary in all Find Me investigations Snyder contacted the lead detective to make certain that they would accept our information as to where Deborah's husband had disposed of her body. Detective Graham was very cordial and quickly accepted the concept of using vetted intuitive consultants to provide location information for Deborah. He indicated in a phone call to Snyder that they had no idea where to look for her body, but he was 95 percent confident that she was deceased and that he knew who killed her. His investigation was stagnated and he welcomed psychic and SAR assistance. He was advised that the group also had available a logistics expert, handwriting expert, canine search and rescue professionals in the event he wanted to use any of those services – cost free, as usual. Graham welcomed the participation of Find Me and AZ-STAR and stated he would provide support in every way possible once any information on Deborah's possible location was provided.

The case was assigned to the Find Me team and the information was forthcoming almost immediately. Twenty psychics received information on the case and all 20 reported that Deborah was deceased. The overwhelming result of the psychics' investigation as to who may have had something to do with Deborah's body indicated her husband.

A few examples from our reports are typical. Keep in mind that the only information the psychics had available was the e-mail alert found at the head of this chapter.

"…They got into an argument at the house, it heated up that's when and where he killed her…the suspect is or was in the military…I feel if he feels pressured he'll try to flee…" Faith Rodriguez

"I am picking up a male type figure, feels like a close connection, like a husband type connection…" Wendy Ishie-Katen

"…this is a domestic case, over finances…he is a vulture and greedy (the ex) he wanted it all. She was very nice and didn't deserve this. She was afraid of him, but didn't think he would do this…" Jacki Spotts

"I feel this man was known to her, there is a lot of violence here, like payback or rage. It has repeated strikes and sick feelings. It was very up close and personal…" Wendy Berkahn

"This (suspect) is someone who is still at large right in the community and is known by many. This man is very familiar to the victim – perhaps the feel of the victim's romantic partner, but things were not good between them at the time of her disappearance…" Danielle Egnew

"…Deborah knew this man because there is this relationship that existed, like dating or an intimate relationship, but definitely she knew him for a long period of time, like most of her life and the nature is intimate or more than friends…" Isaiah Reed

"…I feel the suspect involved is an ex-boyfriend or ex-spouse of Deborah! There is a HEAVY connection to a police department…." Stacey Fields. Fields also named the killer as Robert or Bill/Bob.

"…The rental car pulled up behind her, Bob got out and snuck up behind her and wrapped thin white rope around Debbie's neck and choked her until she passed out…." Lori Neil

"My dream suggests that Deborah Heriford was killed by her husband Harold (aka 'Bob')…" Randall Fawl

The possible locations of her body as determined by the psychics were scattered from one location approximately two hours from Colorado Springs and as close as three blocks from Deborah's residence.

The psychics often get the question, "How can you vary so much in their locations for missing persons?" The answer isn't mysterious or even paranormal. Psychics, just like everyone else, have "on" days and "off" days. A psychic with the flu, facing an emotional crisis, worried about paying the bills, or dealing with a case of the "blahs" just isn't going to perform up to his or her best levels. That's one of the reasons Find Me works with so many psychics on any given case. The more psychics who are "on," the more accurate will be the ultimate determination of any given case.

Note that the psychics are incredibly easy to check out for accuracy. All 20 members who filed reports included GPS coordinates. "If we're off base, it's easy to tell and if we're on, we're right on target and the authorities have a tremendous advantage in search and rescue or search and recovery," Baldwin says.

Kristine Pomeroy's report on the Heriford case is a good example. She wrote, "Pendulum is indicated Deborah is deceased. This was a premeditated murder by someone she knew, and money was the motive. The pendulum is putting her body in Lake Monument about 13 miles northwest of her home. Pendulum is indicated her body is weighed down in the water about 50 feet offshore from east end of Lake. Take Hwy. 25 north to Monument, get off at 2nd Street and take it west to the lake. Coordinate: 39.0526.8"N 104.5241.6"W. Hope this helps."

Snyder contacted Graham, writing, "Our canine partners have been notified and are on standby if you need our assistance in searching the areas we have provided and anything you may have that requires certified cadaver dogs. We also have available a hand writing expert who has testified in court 90 times, both state and federal, identifying deception, personality traits which identify if a person is capable of killing anyone etc. We have a certified police linguistics expert who can uncover similar characteristics and all of these at no charge to your department."

Find Me brings a lot to the table. Graham said to make arrangements and come into Colorado Springs for on-the-scene searches. On June 20, 2012 the Find Me Team and AZ-STAR members arrived to conduct our search. Five canine teams consisting of the handler, one support member and the dogs and eight Find Me members participated. Readers should note that each group is staffed with volunteers, which means everyone showed up on his or her own dime. The expense was a sacrifice in serious time and money, but one these dedicated people make again and again. The cost for this venture was $10,000 and change.

Find Me took this opportunity to bring in a production crew, Looking Up Productions, Inc., to film the search. Their work would provide additional footage of how the teams operate in the field for a documentary the company were in the process of completing. The hotel where the group stayed provided a conference room for use as a command post. Deborah's family showed up for these briefings. On June 21, 2012 the search for Deborah Heriford began.

One of the 25 target areas was Monument Lake in Monument, CO. Kristine Pomeroy's reading identified an area in the lake where she believed Deborah was weighted down and dumped. Snyder, Tomas K. Wind and Katherine Sylvester were assigned to search Monument Lake. Keahi (nicknamed KiKi) a Belgian Tervuren certified in tracking, scent trailing, and cadaver detection was the canine assigned to a team. Keahi was known for her expertise and 100 percent accuracy in locating missing people and the team was excited to have such an experienced animal involved.

The search effort was hampered by an unexpected event. During a break Baldwin, the group's "unofficial-official" photographer, stepped outside to take a few snapshots outside the hotel. He came back in speaking of a small wildfire he'd seen up in the canyons. By the time the next person stepped out for a look, the small fire and grown. This was the beginning of the fierce Waldo Canyon fire, which was the state's most destructive wildfire on record. Nearly 35,000 people were evacuated and the state's second most populous city lost 346 homes. At one point the fire came so close to downtown that the group's hotel was in danger of falling into the evacuation zone. A few searches had to be cancelled because the search areas were burning up. The smoke billow was enormous and the fire's smell was evident even at Monument Lake.

There is a specific methodology on how to conduct a water search and the team was poised to give it their best. The first pass was to put the boat and position Kiki in the area where the wind was coming toward her and also to provide the best conditions for her to do her job. Kiki's first pass was a positive alert in a general area near where Krystine had located her target. Tom and Katherine continued to make numerous passes in that general area and each and every time Kiki would alert that she was picking up the smell of human decomposition. Five passes were conducted to narrow down the area, but it was obvious that something was happening since Kiki alerted on all five occasions. It is customary to follow up with different canine to verify another dog's alerts. Three other canines were brought into the lake area and one by one to execute the same technique and each time the other three dogs alerted on human scent. This, in the world of canine lingo is a positive alert that a human or something human, such as a bloody tampon or bloody Band-Aid is in the water. To take the search to another step the shoreline was searched, which is a method to determine and confirm that the wind is pushing the scent onshore. Every canine alerted on the shoreline where the scent was being pushed in that direction from the suspect location in the lake. At this point, the team believed that they had located something human and perhaps even Deborah's location.

Detective Graham had stated earlier that he would not be available on that date. Obviously, most local resources were being sapped by the fire. He did provide the name and contact information for his partner detective who, according to Snyder, was less than interested. His demeanor that day bordered on being unprofessional and it was painfully obvious he did not want to be there. Snyder attempted to contact this detective on five occasions, but he never responded. This was the precursor to the interpersonal firestorm on the horizon. Surprisingly, the psychics soon learned that his disappointing attitude was shared with Det. Graham. Once contact was made with Graham he stated, "I don't believe in psychic information and I am NOT going to search the lake now or in the future. It is out of my jurisdiction and is more than likely a waste of my time." This was a sudden and a 180 degree change in his (apparent) attitude. A lot of people made a lot of sacrifices to come to Colorado Springs based at least in part on the belief that the local authorities would be cooperating fully with their efforts.

Take a second and flip or scroll back to the head of this chapter and to the Find Me assignment form. Notice the line that reads, "The Colorado Springs Police have asked for our assistance in finding Deborah." The CSPD *invited* the psychic investigators into the investigation.

The teams felt it would have been nice to know his real attitude about psychic information before making the journey. Needless to say they were all shocked. Find Me and AZ-STAR invested 1200 man hours searching for Deborah Heriford. Personal travel and hotel expense was $9000, food and incidentals was $1,100, not to mention five days on the road and for some five days taken off from work. Chrissy and her siblings were also left with the major disappointment of possibly knowing her mother's remains were in the lake and that the Colorado Springs Police Department was not going to do anything about it.

The producer/director of the Find Me documentary, *Pounding the Ground*, who brought her crew in from New York was equally stunned. Denise Goodwin-Pace said, "I know one of the searchers was literally almost killed sliding down a mountain, but managed to save himself at the end. After all of that effort, the detective in charge of the case refused to follow up on the information after it was out of the intuitive sphere and over into what we would call 'the real world' with dogs verifying that information they refused to follow up on that. I find that breathtakingly arrogant. Or stupid. I can't decide which one it is." This was atypical of how Find Me teams have been treated by the police. In 95 percent of the time the police have treated the group fairly and gone out of their way to accommodate them in every way possible. CSPD had essentially stabbed everyone in the back. The fact that Snyder went to great lengths getting permission from the CSPD to film this search (all the way up to the Chief) was a clear demonstration of professionalism and commitment to this project. All the efforts of Find Me and AZ-STAR were potentially a waste of time due to this unforeseen and dramatic change in attitude.

Neither Find Me nor AZ-STAR pitched their tents and left. Arrangements were made with Chrissy to follow up on the search of the lake with someone from the private sector and potentially the Monument Lake Police Department. While at the Lake, Snyder had made contact with several MLPD officers and also the chief of the department with the information about the search and why the group was confident that something of human "decomp" was in the lake.

Denise Pace sums up the entire situation pretty well. "That's hundreds and hundreds of man hours and thousands of dollars in volunteer donations. You have circumstantial evidence. You have the primary suspect moving away. You have the broken-hearted children. And you have somebody like me scratching her head and wondering, 'What was that all about?'"

Snyder sums up the case with an important couple of points. "The significance of the Heriford case is that almost every psychic sending in a report stated that she was deceased and that her husband was the killer. The case is still an open homicide. I believe the Colorado Springs still have him as the prime suspect. He left town right after we showed up. That by itself indicates to me that he was guilty of the crime because he had lived there for 10 or 12 years and his family all lived there. And then right after we came in to do the searches he left the following week and moved to a different state." Some police would consider this a red flag, but CSPD has apparently shelved the case…."

"Murder, in the murderer, is no such ruinous thought as poets and romancers will have it; it does not unsettle him, or fright him from his ordinary notice of trifles."

~Ralph Waldo Emerson

CHAPTER EIGHT: ADRIENNE SALINAS

FROM: KELLY SNYDER

TO: FIND ME

SENT: Friday, August 16, 2013

SUBJECT: FW: NEW ASSIGNMENT – DUE ASAP

Need to know who killed her and suspect(s) location… it has also been confirmed that one body part is missing… provide GPS on that body part if possible.

Kelly

The terms human *remains* and human *body* have entirely different meanings. In a number of searches, Find Me has been asked to locate what is left of what had been a living-breathing human being.

June, 2013 Adrienne Salinas was having a party with her roommates and a group of friends – about 40 people in all. The party started the previous night and was lingering into the early morning hours of the 15th. She was having issues with her boyfriend, Francisco, that night. After he left the party to return to his apartment in Scottsdale AZ Adrienne continued to call him over and over again to the tune of about 14 calls within a span of one hour. The Tempe Police Department confirmed the calls from her cell records. Francisco, who cooperated with the investigation, also confirmed the calls.

Adrienne was somewhat inebriated, but at some point decided to get into her car and drive to see Francisco to resolve the problem.

Unfortunately, about that time the alcohol she had been consuming kicked in and she hit a curve and flattened both of her front ties. She parked on Roosevelt Avenue, and walked the approximately two and one half blocks back to her apartment. She changed her clothing and told her roommate she was going to take cab, apparently still determined to see her boyfriend. She called Scottsdale Cab Guy and a cab was dispatched to a filling station/convenience store approximately two blocks from her apartment. She said she would meet the driver there because there was no room at the apartment complex due to the number of cars in the lot because of the party. She would walk to the convenience store. She called Francisco and stated she was coming to see him.

Scottsdale Cab Guy was owned and operated by Tom Simon who said he sent the cab to pick up Adrienne at the AM/PM gas station near the apartment, but when he arrived he could not find her and went home. The driver was the son of the owner and was also named Tom. There were two phone exchanges between the cab driver and Adrienne, one call for four minutes and another call for three minutes. After Find Me was brought into the case Snyder thought the phone calls were unusual. "What could have been discussed in a seven minute conversation between a customer and a cabby at five a. m. in the morning? This to me is highly suspicious and needs scrutiny in determining 100 percent what was said. I have my theory and would love to hear the cabby's answers," Snyder says.

The phone situation raises other questions. Why didn't the cabby attempt to call Adrienne again to see where she was and why she was not at the gas station? He had just spent nearly half an hour driving to the location, why wouldn't he follow up and attempt to see where she was? His call history would certainly show if he had made such a call.

Simon's presence at the filling station/convenience store is confirmed by video surveillance cameras. He can be seen apparently waiting for someone who never shows up. No one can tell if anyone was inside the cab because all the windows in that company's vehicles are dark glass. You can see out, but no one can see in. After a few minutes, he gets back in his cab and drives off with his customer an apparent no-show. Adrienne had called the cab company about four a.m. and her cell phone went dead at about 5:05 a.m. Adrienne became a missing person. Nothing happened on the case until a grisly discovery two months later in the neighboring town of Apache Junction.

A SWING, A MISS AND THEN SOME HITS

Rarely does a psychic get the full picture with all the details of a case. The information arrives in bits and pieces and that's why the Find Me approach of assigning many psychics to a single case works so well. Still, even the best psychic has off days and will inevitably have misses along with the accurate hits. Any psychic who tells you otherwise is either lying or deluded. Although accurate hits arrived later, apparently, the initial attempts at locating Adrienne were in the misses category.

The Find Me group was contacted by Adrienne's aunt and later by her father and mother requesting the group's involvement in locating the missing woman. Her mother wrote Snyder, "Please HELP US find my daughter… she is a beautiful human being. She is a photographer, loves the outdoors, loves taking road trips and camping. She is mostly quiet around people she doesn't know. She's also silly, goofy, likes to go shopping, loves to read many books, is pretty intelligent and loves to learn…."

AZ-STAR was notified to be on standby for any upcoming

searches in areas identified by the psychic members as possible locations. Find Me members hope to get involved early on to heighten the chances of finding people alive. There were twelve members early on, stating that Adrienne's body could be located at Tempe Town Lake near the Mill Ave Bridge on the North side of the lake. Subsequent searches by police and AZ-STAR were negative. There was little to no interest from the canine searches and even though there were numerous members stating that area was where we would find her, the dogs were saying no. Almost all of the Find Me members working the case believed Adrienne was deceased, but there were no locations other than Tempe Town Lake that put Adrienne in a specific location. This was not the normal response from the members. Snyder was frustrated because for the first time in the group's decade-long history they had no place to look.

Later, the hits started coming in.

Dave Campbell, a forensic astrologer, immediately identified a missing body part.

His report stated, "...missing body part is the head. I feel he put it north of where the body was found...."

Dwayne Brock added, "The head is in a bush along the wash. There are five bushes just south of a dirt road...." A dirt road crosses the wash in the search area, which is lined with significant desert bushes and undergrowth.

Barbara Buck reported, "...I see her in the desert."

Tammy Carpenter reported Adrienne would be found in a "roadside ditch with much brush nearby."

Laura Traplin reported, "The only thing I pick up on a body part is the name 'Canyon Road or Canyon Lake....'"

About 80 percent of the psychics said that she was deceased and that she had been murdered. Numerous suspects were identified or at least partially identified. The most glaring comment was that a high percentage thought that the cab driver was involved. Other than the dispatcher, he was the only one who knew she would be headed in a specific direction to a specific location. Snyder speculates that the driver could be the guilty party in the disappearance. He knew his fare was an intoxicated woman and he decided he would find her on the way to the convenience store and picked her up. "Did you call a cab?" or "Are you looking for a cab?" Obviously, her response would be "Yes."

Here's how Barbara Buck reported on her investigation. "He was driving the Prius cab and she flagged him down. It's not his cab. He couldn't believe his luck. He is a serial rapist and he has a type, girls in their mid to late teens with dark hair. He is an opportunist, doesn't stalk, or anything… this was a rape gone bad. She fought really, really hard, scratched or bit him… he stabs and chokes her. He didn't mean to kill her." Her report is supported by Deborah Voith who filed, "…imaging of sexual assault, cut to foot, gouge to eyes and sense of being rolled, possibly in a carpet."

Marie Hansen's report was similar, "…I can only give you what I feel or see. I believe she has been sexually attacked, but am not sure of the cause of death, but am leaning to strangulation…."

Obviously, anyone working in the psychic investigations arena faces emotional and mental challenges. Find Me psychics work with people when they are at their lowest point in life and most often in tragic circumstances. Who could not be affected? Another challenge faced by many psychics when solving crimes and searching for missing persons is the physical side effects, which can be serious. Alisa Pariette reported, "She tried to fight him off, but he was too strong. My stomach began to hurt as I felt his energy and how scared she was." The physical side effects and the emotional impact of this work has caused a number of Find Me psychics to reluctantly drop out of the group. As one member said, "I experience what the victim experienced. It's too much."

Snyder's scenario, although speculation, fits the known facts of the case. He says, "He could pick her up before going to the convenience store where he more than likely knew there was a video camera. From that point on she is in the cab, under his control, and the windows of all the cabs from his company have blackened out windows. He goes to the store, sits there and then leaves knowing he's been monitored and that no one showed up as a fare. His story is documented as being true that she never showed. He is therefore somewhat off the hook."

The scenario is a perfect example of using crime fighting technology to commit a crime and establish an alibi.

The initial interviews with Simon and his son was conducted by the police. The FBI and other agencies joined the search, but apparently nothing was learned from the additional interviews.

AZ-STAR teams searched Tempe Town Lake because so many psychics felt Adrienne was dumped in the lake or fell in the lake. Several searches of path from the apartment to the convenience store were conducted and the dogs dig pick up her scent, but lost it after about half a block. Based on that, it was indicated that she was picked up or abducted prior to getting to the convenience store. It falls in line with the theory that someone at the party or someone from the cab company was involved – the only people who could know the path she would have taken.

Four searches were conducted of Tempe Town Lake. The dogs did show some interest at the Mill Road overpass, but not a strong indication. This information was given to the police, but Find Me was not contacted regarding any search efforts.

Psychic Hits in the Desert

As previously noted, the initial Find Me reports indicated foul play at Tempe Town Lake, but a number of the psychics pointed to the desert area east of Tempe in the town of Apache Junction.

On August 6th a resident living near Apache Junction was checking his property and noticed buzzards circling in the vicinity of a wash along the west side of Hwy. 88, the road leading to Canyon Lake. His discovery was gruesome: what appeared to be two legs and a torso. The body had been decapitated. He immediately called police. The remains were determined to be Adrienne through DNA analysis. The search for the beloved daughter of Rick and Suzanne Salinas was over. Now came the sadness and puzzle as to why their beautiful daughter was no longer in their lives.

The area in question fit the general description provided by psychic Deb Murray. "The area is very desolate. I do see some tire tracks around which appear to be from ATV type vehicles. There are no buildings around. I see a small mountain range very near. I feel like I had to drive for roughly an hour or so to get to this location...." The wash where Adrienne's human remains were found is about an hour's drive from Tempe and is frequently used by horsemen and ATV riders. It faces the Superstition Mountain range immediately to the east.

Find Me member Barbara Buck reported, "She was wrapped in something that sounds crinkly, like possibly plastic bags or a painting tarp... She was dumped in what looks like a desert wash before the rain. It was dry. The plastic came off after the rain when the river moved her from where she was dumped."

Dr. Randall Fall had reported, "I think the body of ACS was initially left in or near the *Lost Dutchman State Park* (probably on the west side of Hwy. 88 just north of the park entrance.)" Several searches were conducted by AZSTAR with Snyder and Baldwin in their usual roles as "ground pounders" in support. The goal was to find the skull, but the results were negative. Prior to the search Arizona had significant rain storms in that area and if the head was somewhere in that area or wash, it could have been washed downstream. The possibility exists that someday someone walking the wash will find it.

Snyder notes an important psychic hit by Find Me members. "The significance of the Salinas case is that she was decapitated and not one person had made a public comment about that while we were investigating the case. It was assumed her head was removed so she couldn't be identified when in fact everyone knows that DNA testing would reveal her identity.

"A lot of the psychics said that the cabdriver who picked her up was responsible for her death.

"A majority of the psychics said that she was deceased, that a person or several persons from the party were responsible for her death, but ironically about seven or eight psychics pinpointed the cabdriver who said the he was supposed to pick her up, but who said he never saw her. The guestimate from the psychics is that he knew the area – where she was coming from and where she was going – and drove down that street leading to the meet spot and picked her up."

The case remains open.

"It is one of the commonest of mistakes to consider that the limit of our power of perception is also the limit of all there is to perceive."

~C.W. Leadbeater

Chapter Nine: Harold Keeton

FROM: KELLY

TO: FIND ME

SENT: Tuesday, January 10, 2012

SUBJECT: ADDITIONAL ASSIGNMENT

QUICK RESPONSE REQUESTED

HAROLD KEETON

DOB: 05/06/1950

POB: Phoenix, Arizona

TOB:–

Harold drove to 1440 Pinetree Lane – Prescott, Arizona from Phoenix, AZ on Friday January 6th, 2012 – driving a rented red Subaru SUV. His T-Mobile tracking device was activated on January 7th at 4:30 A.M., but shortly thereafter the tracking device went dead. Harold has NOT been seen since. Our SAR has requested to search for Harold, but we obviously need your input as to where we should start looking. Let me know ASAP. Thanks.

Kelly

Sometimes the Find Me investigations are completed, and successfully, in a surprisingly short timeframe.

FROM: KELLY

TO: FIND ME

SENT: Saturday, February 18, 2012

SUBJECT: ASSIGNMENT HAROLD KEETON MEMBERS:

For those of you who worked on the Harold Keeton investigation in Prescott, Arizona.

Mr. Keeton went off the road Hwy. #89 – 150 down into a ravine at GPS coordinates: 34 28 07.03 N 112 30 49.05 W.

There were several members who had the information that Mr. Keeton went off the road on Hwy. #89 and was deceased. One member had the exact coordinates where he was located.

The investigation revealed it was "most likely" accidental.

Thank you,

Kelly

How Close is "Close?" How Good is "Good?"

As Baldwin says, "I'm not always on target, but when I'm cookin' I'm really good." He notes that the pointed tip of his pendulum held over a topological map covers an area the size of a football field. In the scope of things a hit at that point is pretty good, but how good can "good" be? The Find Me record for closest hit probably goes to Dwayne Brock who got about as close as you can get in the Harold Keeton investigation.

Harold "Hank" Keeton, III, a 61 year old man, left his Phoenix home on Friday, January 6 at 11:30 and drove to his vacation home on in Prescott, some 70 miles north.

He left in his 2010 red Subaru Forester SUV. The drive would take Harold from the Saguaro-studded "sky islands" of the Sonoran desert to the spruce and pine covered mountains of higher elevations. The road he took provides beautiful and inspiring views of the ever-changing scenery, but it is also a twisting, watch-where-you're-going experience most of the way. Many of the twists and turns are next to significant drop-offs into washes, ravines and canyons.

Harold suffered from a number of health issues, which had the potential of turning a pleasant drive into a disaster. He made the journey safely, however. Police searchers in the vacation home found numerous clothing items he had taken from Phoenix for the trip. Normally, Harold contacted friends and family to let them know he had arrived safely at his destination, but he did not observe that ritual this trip. When they did not hear from him, his family called his cell phone and other contact numbers, but with no answer.

Harold was soon listed as a missing person.

The case from an outsider's perspective could seem to be fairly simple. The investigators knew Harold's departure point – his vacation house. They also knew he was driving a large, red SUV. Even if he ran off the road somewhere, how hard could it be to spot a big, red vehicle on the side of the road? In this part of the state the answer is "very hard." There are a large number of places where a vehicle could leave the road and crash through a wash, ravine or canyon and slide beneath heavy brush and trees so as to be invisible from the road. Search and rescue pilots often fly directly over the crash site of an automobile, truck or airplane without seeing a thing due to the extremely heavy growth in the area. As it turned out, that was exactly the situation in the Keeton case.

Wendy Ishie-Katen reported Harold in "…a remote, high desert, low forest, small trees or shrubs in area, mountains in back, appears to be a type of canyon off the side of I-17… I do feel it was an accident… I am not feeling any type of foul play…."

Becky Laney reported, "…no foul play. He was driving in the

dark – very dark and drinking something – maybe coffee – not paying attention and not used to the brakes or brake was sticky – not due to a heart attack or illness in his body… hardly knew what hit him….”

Dave Campbell and Dwayne Brock proved to be the most accurate psychics in this case. Campbell reported, “Deceased… off Hwy. 89… trees, just off the highway, I think he may have hung himself, and is a little off the road in the trees….” His report included GPS coordinates for Keeton and his vehicle.

Dwayne Brock reported, “I am getting that Harold Keeton had an auto accident on Highway 89 south of Prescott, AZ. The vehicle went off the road on the left side of the highway and down into a ravine and into a canyon. There is a lot of brush around the vehicle. I am getting that Harold was killed in the accident.” Brock also reported his GPS findings.

In most cases the psychics who are closest to the target on any give case get hits all around what turns out to be the location of the missing person. In this case a different pattern emerged. Three psychics provided GPS coordinates that formed a straight line perpendicular to and crossing Hwy. 89 – Dwayne Brock, Dave Campbell and Kristine Pomeroy. Volunteer pilots flew over the sight following the line. When they were directly over the last coordinate they found Harold's SUV. It was down a canyon and covered in brush – invisible from the busy highway nearby. Dwayne Brock's GPS coordinates were exactly on target – *only one foot from where the SUV was located.*

Snyder says, “The significance of the Harold Keeton case is that we had so many psychics who said he was deceased. Dwayne Brock and Dave Campbell, were within feet of where the vehicle and his body were found. Dwayne's GPS coordinates were 100 percent right on target.

When we're cookin,' we're really good. For Harold Keeton's family and friends that was more than good enough.

"Rosiness is not a worse windowpane than gloomy gray when viewing the world."

~Grace Paley

Chapter Ten: Shawn Fowler, The Family Now Has Closure

"Kelly, Thank you for all your help with our missing person in the City of Perry, Kansas. Our victim Mr. Shawn Fowler was found about an eighth of a mile from his home. He was found floating in the Delaware River within 100 feet of one of the GPS readings your team provided. He was found at approximately 13:45 hours on March 19, 2009. The river had been searched a couple of times by boat and scanner with no results the day prior to the body coming to the surface. Part of the information we concentrated on was the area around a submerged tree as predicted by one of your Team members. I have shared your Team efforts with Deputies, Firemen and Medical persons who assisted in the three month long search. Again THANK YOU ... THANKS TO THE TEAM !!!! The Family now has closure!
Respectfully: Ramon C. Gonzalez, Jr. Police Chief"

Prior to calling in Find Me, Chief Gonzalez was in the position many authorities find themselves when all avenues have been explored and the only course left is to give up or call in non-traditional help. He wrote to Snyder, "I am not sure how to go about this missing person in regards to your organization. Here is a brief summary of events... not sure if you can help. Let me know if you need any further information." Fortunately for Gonzalez and others, the psychics are more accustomed to working with the authorities than the authorities are accustomed to working with psychics. Snyder responded immediately, "Our group can definitely assist you." The case was submitted to the members immediately.

Down to the River

Shawn Folwer was a troubled man – troubled by alcohol abuse and marijuana use. He was tall at six feet, but weighed only 150 – 180 pounds. The drugs dropped his vitamin B and potassium levels, which caused him to at times become confused, disoriented and even delusional. According to one news report, a good friend believed he had gone down to the nearby Delaware River as he did often, but because of his ill health fell in and was overtaken by the cold water. The friend said, "I have gone over to his house and found him down there trying to climb down those steps before with his bad health, and I would get him back up, but I wasn't there this time."

On the evening of December 10th, 2008 Fowler's mother, Judy, stopped by his two-room home. He was sick and confused, so she gave him some Gatorade and three cans of 7-Up before leaving. When she did not hear from him the next day, she called a few friends and neighbors, but no one had heard from her son. The next day she dropped in on the home of Chief of Police Raymond Gonzalez. She said she had not reported him missing earlier because she didn't want to bother anyone in the small town. Perry, in far northeastern Kansas, is seven blocks by seven blocks and is less than a square mile in size. The population is just under 1,000.

Chief Gonzalez immediately contacted County 911 services and activated the local Volunteer Fire Department to conduct a search. Fowler's mother said he never left home without his cell phone and his favorite leather jacket. A search of his home revealed that his cell phone, jacket and checkbook were in the house. He had about $20 on him when she last saw him his mother said. The initial search turned up nothing by the time it was called off at nightfall. On the following day an organized grid search was conducted over an area three miles wide. Sonar equipment was used to search the river and ATVs were used to search walking trails and nearby farms. A Kansas Highway Patrol airplane search the area as well. Again, all results were negative.

The cold weather hampered the search efforts and a second river search had to be cancelled because the river froze over. The sonar unit was put back to use on December 24th and the area near Fowler's home was dragged for his body. The firefighters and other volunteers conducted a second search of nearby outbuildings. Again, the results were negative.

During this time there was no activity on Shawn's checking account or his ATM account. His cell phone showed no activity after December 10th.

THE PSYCHICS CLOSE THE CASE

The standard report notice went out to the members of Find Me, each one applied his or her skills, and filed reports which were compiled and sent to Gonzalez.

Snyder wrote, "The following information is being provided by the psychic members of FIND ME. The individual viewpoints are what each member believes happened on the day that Shawn disappeared. The information is conflicting, but should be considered as separate leads, since each member interprets the information differently. The history of our group's success validates this unique process. This information is being provided for whatever action you deep appropriate."

The information provided turned Chief Gonzalez from an open-minded skeptic to a believer in the value of psychic research. Eight members reported that his body was located in a river or lake or underwater. All reporting members provided GPS coordinates.

Twelve of the 13 reports filed on this case indicated that Shawn Fowler was deceased and a majority of those believed his death to be accidental.

Snyder's report included the following information.

"...his remains are located underwater at or near a bridge in Parry, KS. Further believes that he is near the bank of the river...."

"...his remains can be located at (GPS) in or near Perry, KS... beneath the surface of the water in a river or stream..."

"...(remains in) a catch basin with trees and brush with river nearby or this is a spillover area when river has risen...."

"...remains can be located at or near his residence in the river. His body may have floated downstream and is lodged in some underbrush and submerged trees/debris. Further believes that Shawn's death was accidental...."

"...described as a muddy area with trees/shrubs and water nearby, possibly river, stream or standing water...."

"...further described as a muddy wet area with man-made structure nearby (bridge) or cement structure of unknown origin...."

Patti Rogel filed a report stating, "...I don't feel this was caused by another person/persons. It feels accidental. I don't get any sense of anyone with him at the time he disappeared. I think he slipped and fell."

Daz Smith reported, "...very, very cold. Probably deceased. Felt lower – dropped downwards. Cold, wild eyed expression, a frozen fearful look on his face... the target is located outside in a cold/exposed place. Below or in a lower place... downwards motion is a key theme. Dead in a cold, wet, dark place below the normal level of land...."

Sunny Dawn Johnson's report stated, "…in a body of water close to his house… looks like a river. I feel like he is cloudy minded… not sure if it is drugs, or mental imbalance likely both… but feels like he slips into the water where/near the (GPS) place mark is… feels like his body floated down to where it meets the other body of water…"

The reading from Patty Rogel was right on target. "…Source states that Shawn is deceased and that his remains can be located at (GPS). His remains are in the river near his residence and he is downstream under the water snagged to underbrush/debris. Source believes that he is ¼ to one mile from the above GPS coordinates and provides the following coordinates as also a possibility due to the river currents… further states this was accidental and possibly caused by dizziness which caused him to lose balance…"

On March 19, 2009 the news media reported, "Thursday afternoon proved to be another emotional one for Dale and Judy Fowler. Multiple sources said Thursday that a body found in the Delaware River was believed to be that of their son, Shawn fowler, 44."

About 3 p.m. a fisherman found the body floating in the Delaware River south of Shawn's home.

Psychic detectives are often asked how they endure living and working with such terrible events – kidnappings, murders, and persons gone missing in tragic ways. The answer is that the psychic view in these investigations is focused on the positive aspects of events. It's not so much a matter of seeing the world through rose colored glasses as it is seeing that there are opportunities to help others in ways no one else can help. In this case, the volunteers were able to bring closure to Harold's family, to end their worry and fear, and to bring a level of peace back into their lives.

"When death comes, he respect neither age nor merit.
He sweeps from this earthly existence the sick and the strong,
the rich and the poor."

~Andrew Jackson

CHAPTER ELEVEN: JOSH SZOSTAK

FROM: KELLY SNYDER

TO: FIND ME

SENT: Saturday, May 19, 2012

SUBJECT: NEW ASSIGNMENT – Due May 26th

JOSH SZOSTAK

DOB: 04/12/1968

POB: Troy, New York

TOB: 8:11 a.m.

Josh was last seen at the Bayou Café with his friends on Pearl Street on December 23, 2007. He departed alone at 12 a.m. and was seen by security camera walking north in front of 67 North Pearl Street at 12:15 p.m. in Cosackie, New York.

Please note that I have singled out Josh from the New York College death assignment. Even if you are not going to work on all of the other names, I need for you to work on this one!!!

Thanks

Kelly

LIVE ON CAMERA. DEAD IN THE WATER.

The case was new, but the situation was becoming a familiar scenario to the psychics of Find Me. Josh Szostak a 21 year old man called his family in Latham, NY to tell them he would be going to Albany out for an evening on the town with some friends. He put on a black/greyish hooded sweatshirt with skulls and crossbones across the front, a white t-shirt, jeans and tan sneakers. Josh enjoyed his Guinness beer, but wasn't known for doing drugs and was considered a typical college kid. He was a fairly big guy at 5' 11" and weighing 200 pounds. Josh had a shaved head, but wore a goatee.

By midnight the boys were wrapping up at the Bayou Café on Pearl St. and were about to move on to the next bar when Josh headed to the men's room. When he didn't return, his friends began looking around and even texted him, but without success. Video surveillance across the street caught Josh stepping out of the café. He looked around, used his cell phone, and then moved on. If he was searching for his friends, he never found them. If he was returning to his car, parked back on Delaware St., he never made that connection either.

Josh Szostak was missing.

The local police conducted a search, but when they could find nothing they called in search dogs, but the search was unproductive.

Josh's body was found on April 22, 2008. A boater in Coxsakie found him floating in the Hudson River. His car keys, ID and money were on him and his body showed no indication of foul play or of a struggle. An autopsy was performed at St. Peter's Hospital in Albany and the cause of death listed as drowning. How he ended up in the river was not addressed. Josh's father, Bill Szostak, was far from satisfied with the outcome of the investigation.

One of the curious facts of the case revolves around Josh's cell phone, which was found next to a location from which a state DEC automobile was stolen. The car was found some time later, abandoned and damaged. No fingerprints were found and the DNA evidence was inconclusive. How and why Josh's cell phone ended up there remains a mystery.

Bill, still dissatisfied with the investigation, contacted Dr. Michael Baden, a nationally known forensic pathologist and frequent guest on cable news programs. Baden conducted a second autopsy on April, 28. His results supported the conclusions of the first autopsy.

Baden said, "The investigation as to whether he fell in accidentally because he had been drinking or whether he was pushed in or thrown in by others is really a police investigation matter. The autopsy findings would be the same in either case."

Find Me Sees a Different Picture

Josh's case is still an unsolved mystery and one that leads to an even more frightening scenario. What did the Find Me group have to say about his disappearance?

"...Josh was very sick when he left the bar that night. He was drunk and also under the influence of the 'date rape' drug...." Lisa W.

"...I also got that he was in the wrong place at wrong time not that he was planned...." Debi Bryan

"I feel Josh was walking home from the bar and was drunk. He was smoking and this man asked him for a cigarette – chided him into going down by the water... he then I feel struck Josh in the head and also I feel strangulation...." Brenda Elizabeth Hollander

"...My guides tell me the creep that did this asked him for a cigarette and when Josh turned his back it appears a Taser or stun gun was used on him. I also got a vision of him being tortured...." Rhonda Harris-Choudhry

"...Josh did not know suspect prior to his demise. Josh was blindfolded and carted in bed of suspect's truck soon after he was kidnapped/abducted. Shown some type of head trauma to the victim before victim was transported in Hudson River... Suspect boasted to Josh about leaving smiley faces with/around his victims...." Julie A. Fleenor

"...I meditated and did a reading on Josh Szostak' s pic, making a connection with him and came up with the following information. I feel this was no accident. I got thoughts that Josh was drinking a lot that night he disappeared. Also, I feel Josh was being watched by someone who I feel put something (possibly GHB) in Josh's drink, making him even more intoxicated so they could follow him and take advantage of him as the drug took effect." Josephine Puglisi

"...I see targeted. Being watched, hallucinogenic, paralyzing type drugs. Possibly immobilizing devices, such as a stun gun being used to subdue young men. Groups of attackers, or more than one for purpose or intended act. Van or vehicles with enclosed rear or cargo space. Continue to pick up sadistic secret society...." Beadie Beasley

"...Basically I feel Josh in some way takes responsibility for his demise. What I don't see is how he means this. I can't see if he just dumped himself in the water or he was being reckless... I feel there is something weird about this and a lot of the other cases that seem to be the serial killer type. I'm getting the feeling of a real evil force at work...." Pete Lynn

"...Josh was lured to the water by female – he was pushed/slammed into the river by the male. Josh drowned – without any opportunity to fight back. He did not suffer. This male has murdered before. As many as 19 males and one female...." Jennifer Brazier

"...I feel the death of Josh is related to some of the other college deaths mentioned. I feel there is a type of conspiracy involving many people. Those people belong to a group or cult that may be Satanic in nature... I feel the group members are both male and female. They prey upon certain young men and give them an intoxicant/poison without the victim knowing. The deaths are either from drowning or 'poisoning' but made to appear as a drowning accident due to alcohol consumption..." Joan Hansen

"...I feel like the killers taunted him, and the other victims. I got images, blurry images, as if I were under the influence of drugs… there were two white males taunting me (as if I were seeing what Josh did). They were telling him he was going to die. They were smiling and laughing about it. It feels like they got their amusement from terrorizing a helpless young man, if sober, would have been able to defend himself… it feels like there is a network, or cabal, or other secret association or society of a group of persons who are responsible nor not only Josh, but other murders as well…" Heidi Wright

"…I feel that Josh was drunk and then something was slipped into his drink… I am getting that Josh Szostak was murdered and that this case is tied to the College Serial Murders…."

As with any case, the psychics presented a number of varying scenarios. Yet, as with any case, clusters of clues and repeated themes appeared. A pattern emerged. Josh was drinking heavily and was slipped an intoxicant to enhance the effects of the alcohol and to render him more pliant. He was stunned by a blow to the head or possibly by a stun gun than rendered him unconscious. Josh was murdered and thrown into the Hudson River or he was thrown into the river where he died by drowning.

Josh's case remains open. Snyder remains in regular communication with Josh's father about the continuing efforts of Find Me to bring closure to his case. Hollywood superstar Bruce Willis sponsored a Fund Raiser for Find Me in New York City in November 2014. Bill Szostak attended and spoke eloquently and emotionally about his son and the need for supporting the volunteer efforts of Find Me.

Snyder assured Bill and the audience that the psychics have not given up on solving the mystery of Josh's disappearance and death. Sadly, the Find Me team has discovered that Josh's case is not unique and that teams of serial killers are stalking college age men throughout the country.

"It is an old maxim of mine that when you have excluded the impossible, whatever remains, however improbable, must be the truth."

~Sherlock Holmes (Arthur Conan Doyle)

CHAPTER TWELVE: DARRIN PALMER

FROM: KELLY SNYDER
TO: FIND ME
SENT: Friday, September 10, 2006
SUBJECT: NEW ASSIGNMENT
URGENT – IMMEDIATE RESPONSE
DARRIN PALMER
DOB: 11-20-1965
POB: Phoenix, AZ
TOB: Not Available
Missing Since August 27th, 2006
Please Reply Immediately
Thanks
Kelly

The Darrin Palmer case perfectly illustrates the value of having a number of psychics assigned to a case. Find Me members generally believe that even the best psychic is accurate only about 50 percent of the time. Add to that the fact that often any given psychic will get only a single impression. For example, he or she might get an impression/reading/intuition of the word "four." That word could be a significant clue, but what does it really mean. Does "four" refer to a house number? A street? The floor of a building? The number of victims or perpetrators? A four-leaf clover? If the clue was heard by a clairaudient, could "four" actually be someone shouting "fore" and a reference to golf? Is the missing person on a golf course? Any number of potentially valid and valuable interpretations are possible.

But, add readings from other psychics working on the same case and that single, mysterious clue could become an important piece of the puzzle. Staying with the example here, another psychic could get an impression of a state highway. Alone that clue could remain an unknown, but now suppose there's a state highway number four near the scene of the crime being investigated. Add in another psychic who got the impression of "heading north" and all of a sudden three apparently meaningless clues indicate that the investigators should start looking north on state highway number four. The value of employing psychics is obvious. Thanks to the psychics the search area has been reduced from statewide or larger to a narrow, specific and much easier to research area. That is precisely how everything came together on the Darrin Palmer case. A lot of clues that were hard to interpret individually were pulled together to for a complete picture which led to the successful conclusion of this investigation. What at first could have looked like a set of improbabilities led ultimately to the truth.

* * *

A NIGHTMARE OF A SEARCH AREA

When Darrin Palmer went missing the Phoenix Police Department issued an "Endangered Missing Adult" warning. Darrin was an athletic 41 year old white male, 6' 4" tall and weighing 225 pounds. The circumstances of his disappearance were unknown, but it was assumed that he could be headed to the high country of Arizona in the Payson or Flagstaff area. He took his camping gear with him and he was driving a black 2004 Chevrolet Tahoe which could have easily taken him far into the deep backwoods. The search area was enormous, heavily forested, and crisscrossed with backcountry roads and littered with secluded and hard-to-find camp sites. The area is home to the largest stand of Ponderosa Pine trees in the world. The Coconino National Forest cover 1.8 million acres of land with elevations ranging from 2,000 – 12,000 ft. In terms of search-and-rescue, it is a nightmare. Simply stated, the search area is far too vast and far too thick with growth to search.

PSYCHICS PICK UP THE TRAIL

Darrin's ex-wife, Kathryn, contacted Snyder to request help from Find Me. The standard assignment form was e-mailed and he began compiling the reports as they came in. Individual reports were often highly specific, but sometimes ill-defined in terms of exact location. For example, part of Dave Campbell's report stated, "I am seeing a mountainous area he is on it and can see the mountains surrounding. He is ok. I feel he planned this. I am seeing him fishing in a creek, or small river…"

Mary Clyde's report included, "…a lot of different shades of green; sandy/rocky soil, streambed perhaps, high land, hilly, uneven ground, possibly an old stable or barn nearby, generally north by west of Phoenix... the stable or barn keeps coming up, so it could be associated with an abandoned farm/ranch site or cabin of some kind…."

Those readings were later proven to be highly accurate, but at the time of the search they were only obscure pieces of a much larger puzzle.

One of the psychics intuited a single clue – the number 260. That doesn't sound like much of a clue, but when you look at a map of Arizona's Rim Country you'll see a Hwy. 260 runs through much of it, including one of the target areas – Payson. Still, if Darrin was headed to a camp site, the number of sites and the area to be searched was still enormous. A physical search of such a large area was just impossible.

The sense of urgency was heightened because several psychics felt that Darrin was depressed and even suicidal. Mary Clyde reported, "I got the impression that he was overwhelmed by everything around him… I think he wanted to get away and clear his head and possibly had an accident… I did see him lying face-down with his left arm extended and curved above his head… am not pickup up anything that would suggest that he's alive at this point."

A Find Me member from Australia, Gabrielle "Gabby," who has never been to the U.S. filed a report that later proved to be startlingly accurate. Snyder e-mailed the family the following about her report. "She sees a trading post/store owned/run by an older gentleman. About fifteen minutes away on the highway from the store is a post or pole with red reflector tape. At or near that pole is a narrow dirt road. She believes that Darrin is familiar with this area and the he drove to the end of the road. Of course, she sees tall pine trees and a body of water (believes it's a lake). Where he is located is within 100 - 200 yards of the lake on a high ridge line or knoll overlooking the valley and lake. She further believes that it is within the Payson area… she also came up with the facts that he was depressed and suicidal…."

You can see how the many pieces of the puzzle, regardless of how small or large, begin to form a more complete and accurate picture.

Baldwin filed a report noting a specific target area on the Mogollon Rim east of Payson and north of Hwy. 260 north of Bear Canyon Lake. Although he didn't know it at the time, this area was one of Darrin's favorite camping spots. His pendulum work had Darrin traveling on Forest Road #89.

Darrin's family could not wait for the authorities or official search and rescue parties to begin, so they headed up to the Mogollon Rim to start searching some of Darrin's favorite camping areas. Again, considering the terrain and the vast distances that would have to be covered, this was at best a near-hopeless task. They called Snyder and kept in contact throughout their search.

And their search was successful, tragic, but successful.

They followed the clues provided by the Find Me psychics. They stopped in a store on Hwy. 260 east of Payson. It was run by an older gentleman who remembered someone fitting Darrin's description stopping in to buy a few cans of food. About a fifteen minute drive further down Hwy. 260 the family came to a dirt road headed north. A gate across the road was marked with stripes of red paint. They drove north on the dirt road FR #89 which leads into FR #34, until they met someone coming out of the area. They waved down the driver and showed them the missing person flyer. The driver told them that Darrin had been found that morning. He had camped among a stand of tall pine trees on a knoll overlooking the nearby manmade lake.

Darrin Palmer had crawled into his tent, pulled out his .38 pistol and committed suicide.

Gabby, from Australia, had indicated Darrin's suicidal tendencies. Baldwin remembers filing "seriously injured" on his report. "I remember thinking that he was in need of immediate medical attention. I don't know, but I believe my reading coincided with the timeframe between his pulling the trigger and his death," Baldwin says.

This case is an example of how and why the Find Me philosophy works so well. Psychic research quickly reduced an impossible challenge of a search area into an easily workable search area. In fact, their work led untrained volunteers, the family and friends, directly to the exact location of the missing person. Certainly, some of the psychics were off, some of them way off and that is in the nature of the work. We all have our good days and our bad days and it's the same way with psychics and their work.

When the Find Me team works, there is always a cluster of hits around what turns out to be the location of the missing person. When law enforcement and/or search-and-rescue teams focus on the area within this cluster of a hit, they should have positive results.

Snyder says, "Too often the authorities exhaust all other avenues first and then think, 'Well, we may as well try the psychics.' No matter how improbable it may seem to skeptical authorities, the psychic work of Find Me members has been proven time and again for more than a decade."

And that's the simple truth of it all.

"A liar begins with making falsehood appear like truth and ends with make truth itself appear like a falsehood."

~William Shenstone

CHAPTER THIRTEEN: CALEB ANDERSON

URGENT: PLEASE RESPOND IMMEDIATELY

CALEB ANDERSON

DOB: 7-20-1988

POB: Urbana, IL

TOB: 3 p.m.

Missing from Chino Valley, Arizona (near Prescott) since June 4, 2006 – originally believed to be a runaway, but now considered endangered missing.

Immediate Response Is Needed

Kelly

When is a missing person not a missing person? Every now and then Find Me finds a missing person who isn't really missing and such is the case of Caleb Anderson.

On June 7, 2006 Anderson, a 17 year old, waved goodbye to his parents as they drove off for a business trip two thirds of the country away in the Carolinas. He was considered a good kid and showed no irresponsible tendencies, so Kevin and Diane Anderson became concerned when no one answered a call back home. Although they left a number of voice mail messages, Caleb did not respond. Calls to his supervisors at his job revealed that Anderson had not shown up for work.

Later, Kevin told reporters, "Caleb has a summer job. He's going to be 18 in a month, and we thought it would be a good time for him to get used to being responsible for himself, so we allowed him to stay home."

The worried parents cut short their business trip and returned home to a series of unpleasant and frightening circumstances. Their home had been trashed and their 1994 Chevy Astro Van was missing. Worse, someone had rammed a knife into the center of their couch. They called the Chino Valley Police Department immediately.

Investigators searched the property and discovered Anderson's wallet, money, cell phone, heart medication, and glasses. Apparently nothing other than Caleb and the clothes on his back were missing.

His parents were as confused as the police. Diane told investigators, "It's never like him… He has been very punctual and reliable... Caleb wouldn't do that with the knives." They added that it was inconceivable for him to leave the house without his glasses.

An interesting set of clues indicated that the disappearance might have been a planned event. Several of Anderson's friends said he had made just such a plan and had considered leaving Chino Valley after graduation. He had spoken openly about being called by God to travel to China. Friends said that he wanted to go there to start a revolution in which he would die a martyr. Additionally, he had contact lenses which were missing. Investigators also found an empty bottle of peroxide and hair clippings at the home, hinting that he may have cut and changed the color of his hair.

Even if he had faked his own disappearance, he was still in considerable danger of physical harm without his heart medication.

Kevin Anderson contacted Snyder on June 15th and the case was assigned to Find Me on June 24, 2006. Snyder contacted Detective Vincent Schaan of the Chino Valley Police Dept. to inform him of the group's participation and its commitment to working through the proper channels.

By the end of June the CVPD had pretty much done all it could do with the information at hand. Schaan stated, that "all leads have been investigated to the fullest and have been either eliminated or are still pending due to lack of information. Although more information is available to suggest Caleb left on his free will, there is not enough evidence to rule out all other avenues; therefore all avenues and leads will continue to be explored."

The family's Astro Van was located on Sept. 8 hidden in a pocket of trees well way from the normal traffic flow of hikers, campers and horseback riders in northwest Arizona's Kaibab National Forest. A search of the immediate area was conducted and on Sept. 27th a 12-mile square area around the van was searched. The searches found no evidence of violence or foul play or any sign of Caleb Anderson. Investigators believed that at least one other person must have been involved in the disappearance because someone would have had to have driven Anderson from the van's location.

A handwritten note was found in one of Anderson's school folders. It read, "This is my last will and testament. I, Caleb Anderson, leave all things, possessions, and forms of money to my family, with the exception of my art, and any…" The "last will" was unfinished.

The police had done all they could with the information and resources at hand. That left the searching to the psychics.

Several members reported that Caleb Anderson was alive in the Los Angeles area and that he had faked his disappearance.

Jeanette Healey reported that Anderson was alive. "…someone helped him…another person drove the van for him….a sense of creepiness about a lot of this, not good… it all feels odd…."

Gabriel "Gabby" also picked up on the strangeness of the case. "I don't understand why I keep getting some sort of sick plans or sick game being played to throw people off the track such as red herrings...." Later, he filed a secondary report, which included, "...I keep being struck by a sense of a red herring or deliberate misinformation or deliberate mis-clues to throw people off like some sort of sick game being played. I don't know why, but again I keep sensing this is not a suicide. I also keep feeling that there are lies and deceit, especially from so-called acquaintances of his or friends who are not telling all they know... I sense that he was not in car at time it was left and is a red herring.

Dave Campbell got the impression that Anderson had bleached or lightened his hair.

Amanda reported, "He ran away intentionally...."

Eileen Nelson's report included, "I believe Caleb will be found alive."

Barbe Powell's efforts reveled that Anderson was alive and that, "...it seems things were staged in a certain way, which is rather odd."

Mary Clyde responded, "I don't think the situation is beyond control and that he'll be found OK when he decides to let himself either be found or go home. Got a sense of just needing to be patient while searching."

Baldwin filed what he called a "smash/zoom" report stating that Anderson was alive and physically, mentally and emotionally healthy. "He left voluntarily...."

Nancy Marlowe – "I am getting needles in his arm (drugs? Intravenous? Tattoos?)... I have found that the person is alive and doesn't want to be found or is incapacitated in some way and has an illness or drug problem...."

Peggy Rometo reported that Anderson was in San Diego/Sand Fernando Valley. "I felt like the kid was angry and left... to California and specifically San Diego... I feel like he'll resurface alive in the next 2-3 weeks."

Snyder's report to Detective Schaan said that twelve psychics (one non-member volunteering) stated that Caleb Anderson was alive and seven stated that he left of his own free will. Other details, many of them pertinent to the case were also provided in his report.

Caleb Anderson Comes Home

Anderson called his parents twice on Jan. 1st, 2007 to tell them that he was alive and planned on returning home in the near future. The police traced the call, which came from California.

The case held a few strange twists. Anderson was discovered in the San Fernando Valley area by the children of the family's minister while they were attending a swap meet. This occurred on Dec. 29. Caleb returned to Chino Valley the weekend of Jan. 5th, but, the Anderson family did not notify the authorities until Jan. 8. According to news reports, the reason given for withholding the information, according to Diane Anderson was that "they (the police) didn't ask." She added that he did not want to discuss the matter with the authorities because "he didn't feel he would be believed."

In fact, the minister's children spotted Caleb on Dec. 29th, and the Andersons withheld that information from the police until Jan. 8. They also failed to let police know that Caleb was in Chino Valley over the Jan. 5th weekend.

At this point the CVPD believed the parents' lack of cooperation was approaching the point of hindering the investigation, according to Sgt. Mark Garcia. Had the cause of Anderson's disappearance been known beforehand Snyder would not have initiated the call and the resources of Find Me could have been used to help a family in genuine need. Situations such as this are why the group does not knowingly investigate run-aways.

Find Me expended considerable time, energy, resources and heart in the search for Caleb Anderson. The Chino Valley Police Department estimated that they invested $30,000 worth of man-hours on the investigation. Schaan added that when combined with the efforts of the 30 local, state, national and international agencies involved, the actual cost was in six figures.

"Nine men in ten are suicides."

~Benjamin Franklin

Chapter Fourteen: Steven Ryan Ivens

From: Kelly

To: Find Me

Sent: Wednesday, May 30, 2012

Subject: New Assignment- Due June 6th

Steven Ryan Ivens

DOB: June 14, 1975

POB: Wemouth, Massachusetts

TOB: 8:05 p.m.

Steven left his home at 1701 Scott Rd. #109, Burbank, California on approximately May 11, 2012 and has not been seen since that date. Steven was on foot and did not take his car or have another form of transportation. Burbank PD has requested our assistance in locating Mr. Ivens in hopes that he is still alive.

Thanks…

Kelly

Sometimes, the authorities call on Fine Me to help locate one of their own.

Steven Ryan Ivens was a Special Agent for the FBI assigned to the Los Angeles Field Office. He, his wife and two-year-old son resided on Scott Road in Burbank near the Verdugo Mountains. Ivens had served well with the bureau since September 8, 2008 and before that as a member of the Los Angeles Police Department. He was considered a devoted agent with no record of disciplinary actions taken against him. An avid jogger and hiker, he left the residence wearing casual clothes or athletic gear.

Two facts caused his family and the authorities some concern. Steven was believed to be distressed and possibly suicidal. According to news reports, his wife, Thea, said, "My husband was depressed about something at work, but it was not about his actual job and an FBI agent… He loved his job."

The other factor, a public safety concern, was that his service weapon, a Glock handgun, was missing. There was no evidence of foul play at the home and the investigators saw no indication that he planned on using the weapon to harm others. Still, the potential danger of a distraught man with a loaded gun added a layer of urgency and concern to the search.

An early scent picked up by a search and rescue dog team led to the Verdugo Mountains, a rugged area dense with brush, weeds and tall grass leading to steep cliffs and drop offs. Unfortunately, the scent did not lead to Steven and could have been left over from one of his afternoon strolls days or even weeks earlier. As noted earlier, scent can linger for some time.

More than 100 tips from interested parties, hikers, and neighbors came in, but, as with the scent, led nowhere. Although the Verdugo Mountains seemed a logical place to look, there was no solid evidence that he had gone in that direction, much less to one of the mountain trails.

A massive search and rescue effort was mounted. Agencies involved included Los Angeles County Sheriff's personnel from Altadena, Montrose, Santa Clarita, and Sierra Madre Search and Rescue teams, the Special Enforcement Bureau-Emergency Services Detail (paramedics, bloodhounds. Off-road vehicles, and a helicopter, and air, ground and canine units with the Burbank PD, Glendale PD,

LAPD, Long Beach PD, Los Angeles City Fire Department, and the Los Angeles Fire Department, the Ventura County Sheriff's Department, and the Burbank Airport PD. Teams consisting of up to 40 FBI agents at one time worked with the various teams.

The searches continued for weeks, but without results and the hunt was called off. Thea Ivens refused to give up. That's when Snyder received the following:

> *Hello. I'm Steve's wife, Thea Ivens. His disappearance was on the news a couple of weeks ago. However, the law enforcement agencies had actively stopped looking for him because they couldn't find him... I'm determined to find him. I felt that they didn't thoroughly search the Verdugo Mountains. If he's still out there, we need to find him. I would really appreciate any response... Thank You.*

That's when the call to Find Me went out. When the reports were in, Snyder filed a single report to Detective Brian Gordon of the Burbank PD. Snyder included a brief note as to how to evaluate the information.

"The following information is being provided by the intuitive members of FIND ME. The individual viewpoints are what each member (source) believes happened on the day of Steve's disappearance. The information is conflicting because each member interprets their information differently. It is our intent and belief that the leads provided within this report will identify Steve's location based on the history of our successes and for whatever action you deem appropriate."

Twenty psychics reported that Steve was deceased and eight of those provided GPS coordinates. Twelve stated that he was a suicide. Three members believed he was alive.

Here is a sample of their responses. These are only extracts. The full reports contained significantly more information, such as motivation and detailed descriptions of the area around their GPS coordinates.

Julie F. – "Mr. Ivens was shown with overwhelming sadness as well as showing signs of being extremely despondent walking from his home north along Scott Road. Strong awareness of suicide intention with drugs (prescription it seems), feeling no hope for life… Very strong energy feeling that victim felt he had tried so hard all of his life to make a difference, but just didn't feel that he belonged… Victim left his residence, on foot, and walked to his final destination in the somewhat hilly area directly behind the church parking lot of St. Francis Xavier Catholic Church…."

Beadie Beasley felt that Steven was alive, but being held against his will. The location was "near a church." The word "catholic" came up in the reading.

Rachael Schmidt – "Steven was very distraught when he left his apartment. Confused about a situation he has gotten himself into… Steven has pills and considered suicide….

Michelle Beltran – This was an accident of some kind, but also suicide feels connected to it."

Laura Trapin – "I feel he was depressed and committed suicide… I feel he had a gun… lots of adrenaline rushing."

Wendy Ishie-Katen – "I'm feeling some sadness from him… stress, his energy is very unstable… I don't feel he is alive… I am seeing alcohol again and a gun. He may have stopped off at a bar or someplace to pick up alcohol… I feel like he was also in a situation. I am hearing "too deep." He feels like he just gave up… I am hearing, "What is the point?" Even though I am getting a couple of scenarios going back and forth, I do feel that he committed suicide… I am seeing a male with a gun to his head and pulling the trigger...."

Heidi Wright – "I think he is deceased. I get a feeling this is suicide… He was wearing running or exercise attire (shorts, running shoes, etc.) I believe he also had a gun with him. I see this gun as being dark in color, semi-auto, and very light weight, like perhaps a plastic or polymer stock like a Glock or Taurus… I don't actually see him shoot himself, but I have a feeling that is what happened…."

Bobbi New – "From the information I have received – when he is finally found he will be deceased…."

Danielle Egnew – "Mr. Ivens appears to have been suffering from depression. I see him very emotionally distressed on the inside… If Mr. Ivens is alive, he has experienced some sort of severe break mentally. Unfortunately, I believe him to be deceased. Because of his mental status at the time of his disappearance, I believe Mr. Ivens took his own life."

Dave Campbell – "His chart shows clearly he was depressed and suicidal. The timing was triggered for suicidal thoughts… He planned the suicide…."

Mark and Maggie Stark – "Mark felt he was suicidal, depressed, he was involved in too many things. Couldn't cope with his life… Both felt pain in our heads, possible gunshot…."

Dan Baldwin – Although Baldwin was one of the few who felt Ivens was alive at the moment, he reported that the agent was "under extreme mental stress and there is concern that he is 'cracking up'…"

Dwayne Brock – "I am getting that Steven shot himself…."

FIND ME GOES TO BURBANK

Find Me and AZSTAR scheduled a multi-day search for Steven beginning July 21, 2012. Six members of AZSTAR with three dogs were involved. Snyder and Baldwin represented Find Me.

Most psychic hits were in Ivens' neighborhood and the nearby Verdugo Mountains. The mountains have hiking trails, but off-trail areas are extremely overgrown with dangerous drop-offs. Some areas are impossible to explore by "ground pounding" and would require special repelling equipment or even search by helicopter. Additionally, the area is inhabited by mountain lions and, as the team Baldwin accompanied discovered, rattlesnakes.

Daily searches lasted from sunup to sundown, with different teams shuttling from one GPS site to another. Because of the terrain and the complex layout of the streets, overpasses, and drainage ditches, progress was slow.

The complex street layout caused one of the greatest frustrating episodes experienced by the Find Me ground pounders. Snyder and Baldwin and an AZSTAR team were checking out several GPS locations on the last day of the search. It was a very physically challenging day made more challenging because the GPS system the team used as a roadmap continually led them to dead ends where through streets were indicated. As they were looking for the final psychic hit, a specific GPS location, the system led them to another dead end. What appeared to be a through street stopped at a large, fenced in drainage channel.

Because the sun was rapidly going down and rerouting would mean searching in the darkness, the search for the day – and for the week – was ended. With only one site left to search, the teams had to call it quits. Find Me and AZSTAR returned home without finding Steven Ivens.

Body of Missing FBI Agent Found in Burbank

Two hikers found Steven's remains on July 31, 2012. They were walking in the Verdugo Mountain foothills on Scott Road when they noticed a suspicious odor. The police were called. A weapon was found at the scene and the body was tentatively identified as Steven Ryan Ivens, an identification later confirmed.

The remains were found near St. Francis of Xavier Catholic

Church, a location specifically mentioned by one of the Find Me investigators.

Flip back up a page or two and you will notice the excerpt from the Beadie Beasley reading contained "near a church" and the word "catholic." The report from Julie F. was even more specific with, "his final destination in the somewhat hilly area directly behind the church parking lot of St. Francis Xavier Catholic Church...." Julie's report listed a GPS coordinate.

This was that last location the team Snyder and Baldwin were with could not get to because of the blocked through street. With a little more daylight or a more accurate GPS reader, the mystery of Steven's location could have been solved while the teams were in Burbank.

Sometimes even when everything "clicks" into place, circumstances intervene to produce a less than hoped for resolution. But the bottom line is still a positive one. Steven Ivens was located and the value of psychic investigation has been once again proven.

"Suicide is what the death certificate says when one dies of depression."

~Peter D. Kramer

Chapter Fifteen: Howard Hall

From: Kelly

To: Find Me

Sent: Thursday, March 11, 2010

Subject: New Assignment

Response Due: March 18, 2018

Howard Hall

DOB: 12/14/1939

Howard Checked out of the Drifter Motel in Silver City, New Mexico on June 30, 2009. His truck was located on July 17th, 2009 at (GPS coordinates) on Hwy. #78 Near the Arizona/New Mexico border. It was determined that the truck had been sitting there for the entire three week period since he checked out of his motel.

Howard Hall was apparently depressed over not being married or having kids. Friends indicated that he was unhappy with his life and was going to New Mexico to check it out and to see if he would like to move to "the land of enchantment."

He stayed at the motel in Silver City for just over a week and then left town, never to be seen alive again. His locked vehicle was found in a creek bed on July 4th along Hwy. 78 by the Grant County Sheriff's Office. Howard's truck license plates were expired and a citation was issued – the only official action taken that day. The GCSO checked the truck periodically and on July 19th deputies noted that the rear sliding window had been opened. The office ran the plates again and discovered the owner was listed as a missing person.

The state police were notified that afternoon and the vehicle was towed to Silver City. The tow truck operator was a former Search and Rescue field coordinator who by training automatically analyzed the scene when he arrived. The truck bed contained Howard's personal property protected by a tarp. Other personal belongings were neatly placed on the passenger's side seat and his partial dentures had been placed on the dashboard – indicating the actions of someone in a depressed or possibly suicidal frame of mind.

According to Howard's cousin, Howard was not a long distance hiker and would certainly not go hiking off trail.

A New Mexico search and rescue mission was initiated and cadaver dogs were put into the field. The teams, hiking and using ATVs, searched an area within a radius of ¾ to one mile of Howard's truck. The area was rugged and contained many crevasses, many of which could not be searched in safety.

The initial search was unsuccessful.

Some of Howard's friends and family discovered the Find Me website and contacted Snyder. At that time the membership of Find Me had grown to 80 members and they were immediately called into action.

About half of the group responded, with the vast majority saying Howard was deceased. Here is a sample, excerpts, from some of the reports.

Linda Blume – "Will the police find Howard? Yes, after an extensive search and agencies working together."

Daz Smith – "A large rd./highway that forks with a smaller rd. just ahead. A river creek is also in the area." (GPS coordinates provided with Daz's report.)

Dan Baldwin – “Deceased/murdered.” (GPS coordinates provided with Dan’s report)

Stacy Nelson – “I feel like Howard was trying to work towards getting his life in order… Wasn’t sure if he could reach his hopes and dreams.”

Catherine McKenna – “I feel a gun was involved.”

Andrea Mackenzie – “I saw a gun. The victim was also struck in the head.”

Patti Rogel – “I believe Howard left his vehicle of his own accord just short of reaching the Arizona border. I feel he was alone and no foul play was involved by another person or persons. I also believe that he is deceased and his remains can be found within a 2 ½ mile radius of where his vehicle was left of Hwy. 78….”

Donna Reid – “…(I) hear ‘I am stupid’ and ‘stupid, this is stupid.’”

Alisann Smookler – “He is only 1/2 miles from his car.”

Twelve psychics provided GPS coordinates in the vicinity of Howard’s truck.

According to Find Me protocol, Kelly contacted the Grand County Sheriff’s Office and the New Mexico State Police with the information, including the GPS coordinates, but no one responded.

Howard’s skeletal remains were discovered and positively identified April 19, 2010 approximately three miles from Silver City, NM off Hwy. 78 within 1,000 yards of where Dan and Daz had placed him in their reports.

Snyder was interviewed by the Silver City Sun newspaper about the incident. He said, “It looks like they (the searchers) did one hell of a thorough job. They just didn’t go far enough.”

To borrow a popular phrase, whenever someone is missing, when friends and family members are worried, when the authorities need our help, the Find Me members are always willing to go the extra mile.

"The thief to be most wary of is the one who steals your time."

~Anonymous

Chapter Sixteen: Jaycee Lee Dugard

From: Kelly

To: Find Me

Sent: Sunday, August 19, 2007

Subject: Re: Jaycee Lee Dugard

This Is A Voluntary Assignment

The FBI agent, Police Detective and a California Search & Rescue individual who have worked on this investigation since she went missing have asked our group to look into this case.

Response Due: August 27, 2007

Jaycee Lee Dugard

DOB: 05-03-1980

POB: Waiting

TOB: Waiting

Missing since June 10, 1991 from S. Lake Tahoe, California

While walking from her residence to the bus stop the step-father observed a vehicle with a male and female in the vehicle stop and the female grabbed Jaycee and put her in the vehicle.

A 1979-1980 gray Ford or Mercury two-door sedan was the vehicle used in the abduction.

Respond by August 27th….mark your calendar.

Kelly

The incredibly brutal acts perpetrated on the nation's children are shocking, horrifying, and heart-breaking. It is a little-discussed area of our culture in which Find Me members are often to called explore.

KIDNAPPED IN BROAD DAYLIGHT

Jacyee was 11 years old on June 10, 1991. She was wearing her favorite pink outfit when she left her house to walk uphill to catch the school bus. As she got halfway up the hill a gray sedan approached and stopped. When the window rolled down a man shocked her into unconsciousness with a stun gun and dragged her into the car where a woman held her down. Jaycee's step-father, Carl Probyn and several of Jaycee's friends were equally stunned. They watched in horror as the car drove away. Probyn grabbed a bicycle and gave chase, but soon the vehicle was out of sight.

The story was big and almost immediately local and national news organizations picked it up and assigned reporters and crews to South Lake Tahoe. Search efforts involved concerned neighbors and citizens and virtually every law enforcement and related resource in the community. Terry Probyn, Jaycee's mother spearheaded numerous efforts to keep her daughter's disappearance in the public eye. Child Quest International and the National Center for Missing and Exploited Children joined the campaign. Posters, fliers, t-shirts and even a song, "Jaycee Lee," were used to keep the search efforts alive. The television program *America's Most Wanted* featured her story in June of that year.

Jaycee would remain missing for 18 years, living the life of a tortured sex slave who gave birth to two children while in captivity.

A LIFE OF CAPTIVITY

Jaycee was kidnapped by Phillip Craig Garrido, 58, and his wife, Nancy Garrido, 54. It is believed that Nancy Garrido stalked Jaycee and wanted her as a prize or a gift for her husband. After kidnapping her, they handcuffed their prisoner, covered her with a blanket and drove to their home in Antioch, CA, a couple of hours away from South Lake Tahoe.

As soon as they arrived Phillip Garrido forced his prisoner to take a shower with him. Jaycee was still in handcuffs the first time he raped her.

Garrido had a track record of such crimes. In 1976 he had been convicted in South Lake Tahoe of the kidnapping and rape of Katherine Calloway. Tried in state and federal courts, a psychiatric evaluation found him a sexual deviant and a serial drug abuser. He should have been high on the list of suspects.

Jaycee was kept in a locked room. She was pregnant by the age of 13. Her first daughter was born in August, 1994. Her second daughter was born in November, 1997. At some point in her captivity, it is believed that Jaycee became a victim of the Stockholm syndrome, a situation in which the kidnap victim exhibits empathy and positive feelings toward the kidnapper. Eventually, she was kept in a back yard which included sheds (one soundproofed), two tents, and a camping-style shower and toilet. These features were protected from view by a six-foot high fence, tall trees, tarps and other outbuildings.

Law enforcement visited the home twice, but never asked to see the back yard. This was the first of many failed opportunities throughout the years to find and rescue Jaycee and her children – failures in protocol, lapses of judgment, and a lack of common sense.

Jaycee Found

In August, 2009 Phillip Garrido visited the offices of the San Francisco FBI where he dropped of an essay about religion and sexual activity. He then visited the University of California Berkley police office with his two daughters to get permission to host a "God's Desire" presentation on campus. Campus officials thought Garrido's actions were erratic and that his daughters seemed overly sullen and submissive. Things just didn't seem right. He was asked to come back the next day. A campus official notified the local police who unearthed the fact that Garrido was a registered sex offender on parole for kidnapping and rape.

When Garrido returned the next day, a police official sat in on the meeting. Because there was no cause for an arrest, but much cause for concern, the officer left a message with the parole office. Agents began investigating him and his bizarre behavior. He was ordered to appear at the parole office in Concord, CA. Garrido, Nancy Garrido, Jaycee and her two daughters arrived. Jaycee answered to the name Allissa.

The women and girls were separated from the male. During the interviews things just weren't adding up, so the Concord police were called in. Garrido finally confessed that he had kidnapped, raped and held Jaycee captive. He and his wife were arrested. Jaycee and her parents were soon reunited. She was in good health and in good spirits. An aunt said her daughters were, "…clever, articulate, curious girls who have a bright future ahead of them."

Phillip and Nancy Garrido pleaded guilty of kidnapping, rape and other charges in April, 2011. Phillip Garrido is serving time at the California State Prison, Corcoran. Nancy Garrido is paying her dues at the Central California Women's Prison.

Find Me Heats Up a Cold Case

Find Me does not usually take cold cases for the basic reason that there are always current, on-going investigations and a stack of recent disappearances and unsolved crimes waiting to be investigated.

Some cases, however, cannot be ignored, especially then the FBI, local law enforcement and other interested persons call. In the case of Jaycee Dugard a break in protocol was called for. Snyder answered,

"Normally we would not work on a case this old because of all the current fresh investigations that are ongoing. I will, however, run it by our board of directors and see what they say."

Snyder brought the matter before the board. The members voted unanimously to accept the assignment.

Ten reports were filed regarding Jaycee Lee Dugard deceased. These were forwarded to Sgt. Brian Williams of the South Lake Tahoe Police Dept.

"The following information is being provided by the members of the Find Me Group. Each source has provided what they believe happened on the day of Jaycee's disappearance. This information is being provided for whatever action you deem appropriate."

Six of the ten responding psychics reported Jaycee deceased. As usual, the responses were "all over the board," but many of the psychic hits were on target.

Baldwin reported that, contrary to popular belief at the time, Jaycee Dugard was alive, aware of who she was, and that she was being held against her will. He also reported visualizing images of a circular structure something like a corrugated metal water trough under a shed or roof. (Garrido had an above ground swimming pool and sheds in the back yard.)

Gabrielle "Gabby" reported a sense that Jaycee was abducted, that she had been stalked and that the abduction was planned. "The two people have done many crimes together and I do sense pedophilia with the male and the woman along with it… there is a gap of time between crimes, but a different aspect to this crime, was kidnapping and sexual in nature and an obsessional quality with young girls and innocence of girls… there is a history with the man I kept sensing mug shots and a prison sentence and a sense of criminal acts of violence… I kept getting a Christian cross and really strong ideas about women but they were sick and felt like he was going on and on in his mind about innocence of women. Something to do with bible verses...."

(Nancy Garrido stalked Jaycee as a prize for her husband. His twisted religious nature is evident in his "God's Desire" program and other related statements and actions.)

Trisha Dolan filed that the abduction felt "staged," adding, "It is so odd that I do NOT get "dead," just a new life."

Teresa Dyke reported Jaycee as alive. "I feel like this guy just doesn't kill children."

Keep in mind that these reports came in 18 years after the kidnapping at a time when virtually all concerned believed Jaycee had long since died.

Although Lauralyn Harter felt that Jaycee was deceased, she reported other, helpful information. "I feel she was kidnapped by a couple – the woman did it for the man. Her "partner" was into young girls. I feel she was molested and kept as a servant. I feel like they locked her in a room in the house...."

There are sound reasons for the Find Me protocol against taking on cold cases. There are equally sound reasons that call members to go above and beyond and to take on additional, and often emotionally challenging, cases regardless of the timeframe involved. Although Jaycee did not attend the Garrido trials, she did send a message to be read in court. Her words sum up why the Find Me members feel their work on this case was worth the extraordinary effort.

Her message read in part:

> "*...Phillip, I say that I have always been a thing for your own amusement. I hated every second of every day of 18 years because of you and the sexual perversion you forced on me. To Nancy, I have nothing to say. Both of you can save your apologies and empty words. For all the crimes you have both committed I hope you have as many sleepless nights as I did. Yes,*

as I think of all those years I am angry because you stole my life and that of my family. Thankfully, I am doing well now and no longer live in a nightmare. I have wonderful friends and family around me. Something you can never take from me again. You do not matter anymore." Jaycee Lee Dugard

"Ours is the century of enforced travel of disappearances. The century of people helplessly seeing others, who were close to them, disappear over the horizon."

~John Berger

CHAPTER SEVENTEEN: MIKE GREFNER

FROM:KELLY

TO: FIND ME

SENT: Friday, February 17, 2012 7:17 a.m.

SUBJECT: NEW ASSIGNEMENT – Due February 23, 2012

MIKE GREFNER

DOB: MAY 18, 1977

POB: Red Deer, Alberta Canada

TOB: Unknown

Mike was last seen at 8537 Rope Tow Way, Whistler, Canada on January 17th, 2012 at 2 a.m. confirmed by a cab driver that personally knows Mike and dropped him off at the above address.

Thanks,

Kelly

Mike was a positive and well-liked young man who was in town in an attempt to take the next step up in his career as a DJ. One of his friends, Gary Tennant, said, "He was extremely well-loved for what he was and what he did. He was always down-to-earth and always looked on the positive side of things."

Mike and his buddy, Cedryk, showed up at Garfinkel's Night Club in Whistler about midnight, Monday January 16th. They checked their coats and Cedryk went to the restroom. When he came back Mike was no longer in the club. Cedryk stayed at the club until it closed, but Mike never returned. Cedryk texted him at 2 a.m., but Mike did not respond.

No one knows why, but from one a.m. until two, he was driving around with a cab driver named Don Eagleton. The time is well-established because they showed up at Sara Baker's house at 1 a.m. while she was asleep. He spoke to her roommate saying he had lost his wallet and then got back into the cab. The roommate said he appeared "wasted."

At 1:10 a.m. the pair went to Garfinkel's to retrieve his coat, but he never got it. Tennant said that the night his friend disappeared was one of the coldest that winter – an uncomfortable and potentially dangerous situation, particularly for someone drinking heavily.

Apparently, Mike continued his habit of making late night, drunken phone calls, but he never got his coat. He made a number of calls and texts between 1:15 and 1:40 a.m. While driving around, he and Eagleton also stopped and spoke with people at a number of bus stops. Eagleton took his passenger to Mike's home at 1:58 a.m. where he helped him to the door. Inside, Mike got money to pay for the ride from a substantial stash he kept behind the clothes dryer. Mike made or attempted to make more calls, the last apparently at 5:10 a.m.

That's the last confirmed sighting/contact with Mike Geffner, although an unconfirmed report indicated that a waitress had seen him and a woman at a café in Pemberton, which is about 20 minutes north of Whistler. The woman, a waitress, was shown a video of Mike and she was confident that he was the man she had seen.

At the time, Mike was temporarily living at the home of a friend, Robyn. His place was a mess, but there were no indications of a struggle and no indication that anything of value had been taken. Friends became worried when Mike did not show up for his shift at

Maxxfish on Wednesday evening. The Royal Canadian Mounted Police were called. A check of Mike's place revealed $1400 in his hidden stash behind the clothes dryer. According to his mother, Katherine Gefner, this money soon disappeared, a fact that has not been investigated to her satisfaction.

A curious incident occurred on the previous Sunday night. Mike had just met a woman, Sarah. He was at her house that night and about 1 a.m. (Sunday) had received a phone call. She heard someone on the other end of the line yelling and observed Mike trying to smooth things over. She could tell he was disturbed by the incident.

Desperate, Katherine turned to a number of psychics she found on social media, but, in her words, they only led her on "wild goose searches." Others believed that Mike was alive, but hiding out because he "needed space" away from everything for a time.

After a month of futility and heartbreak, she found the *Pounding the Ground* documentary about Find Me, which led to her writing Snyder.

FIND ME SEES OVER THE HORIZON

The psychics were able to contribute substantially to solving the case. Although the results were not what the family and friends were hoping for, the group at least provided answers and closure. All, but one member, reported that Mike was deceased. Eight provided GPS coordinates within one half mile of where his body was located.

In mid-March the RCMP confirmed that the body of a man found in a wooded area approximately ¼ mile from his home near Alpine Meadows was Mike. An autopsy was performed, but a representative of the RCMP, Staff Sgt. Steve LeClair, stated that it did not provide a cause of death. He added that there was no evidence of suicide or foul play and that a toxicology report had been ordered. "We're still trying to determine what happened," LeClair said.

Psychics Dwayne Brock and Wendy Ishie-Katen provided the most accurate reports. Brock said that Mike was deceased. Each provided GPS coordinates.

Brock's report included, "I am getting that Mike is on a dirt trail or pathway just west of Valley Dr. I am getting that Mike passed out in this area and that he froze to death and that his body has been cover by snowfall."

Ishie-Katen filed a detailed report that stated in part, "… it feels as if he was approximately ½ mile from his home… I do not feel that he is alive… I'm hearing 'losing it all.' He may be an alcoholic or drinks heavily… it feels as if he was contemplating suicide, yet it also feels accidental… there's a path around this area. Maybe not a formal path, but it appears like a dirt path or a tiny road. I heard the word 'trail.'"

Others added pieces to the puzzle. Many of them provided details physical descriptions of a wooded area.

Heidi Wright – "My attention was drawn to the area behind the house… I do feel he is behind the house as you are facing the front of the house. I think he is within a relatively short distance of the house, like within one mile and probably more like ½ mile."

Lenora Shortt – "He sat down by a tree and went to sleep. He never knew he had passed away by hypothermia."

Shawn Marie Conner – "I'm not sure the suspect is dead, but I'm leaning in that direction… I felt nauseated, dizzy like drugs/intoxication, then pain in my stomach."

Dave Campbell – "Deceased… I feel he was extremely intoxicated/drunk…."

Laura Traplin – "… I hear that Mike Grefner was highly inebriated… I hear he did have a head wound, but died of hypothermia."

Pam Forseth – "Suicide/accidentally. He is very lost right now. He's not too sure what's happening… 'tell mom and dad I love them and am very sorry…."

Martin Ollier – "Subject arrived and felt the need to go out… ill prepared for the environment due to an unsettled feeling within his gut to contemplate events and discussions from earlier… became confused and disoriented... a confused state of mind."

Wendy Berkahn – "I get like an alcohol feeling like drunk."

Danielle Egnew – "I feel he is within 1 – 3 miles of the house. I believe he went out on a hike, last minute, perhaps even a little recreational alcohol or drug use (marijuana) and encountered difficulties while out on the hike – either lost or turned around, but there is an outdoor calamity here involving snow, freezing, water, disorientation. This feels like hypothermia, and I believe the missing person felt he was an 'outdoorsy' type, however, was rather ill prepared for being lost, or being injured, in the snowy woods. He may have been feeling extra confident from the drugs or alcohol about the hike."

As with any investigation some reports were off base. For example, Baldwin had him located in the sewer system in downtown Whistler. Another psychic reported that she was just "blocked" on the case and couldn't come up with any information. And one other was suffering from a sinus infection, which prohibited accurate reading at the time. Still, the bottom line for Find Me is success. The psychics accurately noted that the young man was deceased. Many provided GPS coordinates close enough to Mike to narrow a search area. Many provided accurate physical descriptions of the search area, too. And a majority of the reports were accurate as to the probable cause of death – hypothermia due to inebriation.

Mike Grefner did "disappear over the horizon," but thanks in large part to Find Me volunteers that disappearance and the heartache of not knowing it brought on, came to a swift end.

"Well done is quickly done."

~Julius Caesar

Chapter Eighteen: Brendan Davis

Find Me members want police and other authorities to consider them as first responders because when they get involved things can happen fast. The case of Brendan Davis is a perfect example.

Caralyn Davis, the mother of a missing young man sent Snyder at missing persons flyer with a note stating in part, "We need your help! I need your help finding my son Brendan Davis who went missing on 4/27… I would love any help, advice or consulting with our Detective at UMASS Boston. Boston PD who filed the report have been absolutely useless in helping us."

Brendan's mother was desperate. All efforts to find her son had proven fruitless. The group went to work immediately.

Branden Disappears

In late April, one of Brendan's friends received a confusing and disheartening letter.

> *Here is the poker money I was holding onto for you. Also, the keys to my apartment. The rent is paid through the end of May. And August is already covered. Feel free to use it as your Boston home for the summer. Take care and good luck.*

He also wrote to another friend asking her to take care of his cats while he was away. Clearly, the young man was planning on an extended trip.

Branden left the apartment without travel luggage or extra clothing and only $180 in cash. He left his cell phone, but took the sim card. He also left his Massachusetts driver's license and student ID.

The family was worried sick. This type of behavior was unusual and certainly not expected. Caralyn Davis said, "We're a tight-knit family. We're very concerned." His former girlfriend said, "I think he was very much a level-headed and intelligent person who struggled with psychological issues. But this was very unexpected." His employer was also puzzled by the sudden disappearance and told reporters that the young man was reliable and the two years he had been employed were without incident. Bill Weigele, his supervisor, said, "He was a very well grounded, very level-headed, again not your typical devil-may-care college student."

Caralyn and her husband, Steve, flew immediately to Boston from their home near Denver to begin searching.

Find Me Appears

Caralyn e-mailed follow up reports to Snyder which shed light on possible motives for the disappearance.

"I know he was depressed and angry about the 'mistakes' he had made with his life and education and investing too much time and energy into another girl who broke his heart and holds himself responsible for being too controlling. Brendan wanted to rid himself of what he considered bad habits – namely controlling everything, being OCPD, drinking too much, doing things that were not acceptable to his character. Brendan is a perfectionist and too bright for his own good. Love that boy, but he is a challenge."

Twelve psychics reported that Brendan was alive, living in New York City, and was not in any danger. GPS coordinates were provided as were physical descriptions of the area where he was staying, and even locations where he could be found, such as the local library.

Typical of the reports are:

Lisa W. – "Mr. Davis needed a mental vacation and is resting in a friend's apartment in NYC. He'll resurface in his own time."

Alex Stark – "He is living in NY to get away from it all."

Adrea Peet – "I believe that Brendan is alive and in an area hospital in Manhattan, NY… "Does not want to put a burden on (his) family."

Amy Utsman – "I feel Brendan is alive… He is a nice kid just trying to find himself…."

Tammy Carpenter – "(in New York City) May be spending time at homeless shelters or public parks up to 20 blocks away from the library."

Patti Rogel – "I believe Brendan is alive. I do not believe he met with any foul play. It is my opinion that he left of his own accord… I did not feel he would deliberately hurt his mother this way."

Anya Briggs – "I think this guy wants to be an actor or performer of some sort. Loves New York, wants to 'find himself' and to be 'freer than he's ever been' – no commitments, forget the life he had before and lust live by the seat of his pants. He is very much okay and not in danger."

Note that in addition to the locations provided, the psychics also picked up on Brendan's mental state and possible motivations for leaving in such a manner. Some of the psychics even noted the guilt felt by the young man for his actions.

According Find Me protocol, Snyder worked with the local authorities. The information gathered was then provided to Caralyn and Steve Davis.

With this information in hand, Bredan's father traveled to New York and found his son the next day.

Note to parents, friends and authorities involved in missing persons cases: vetted psychics were and are available for immediate service. So, why wait for, "Well, we've tried everything else; we may as well try the psychics."

Take a cue from Caesar. Well done is quickly done. Why wait?

"Close, but no cigar."

~Famous Saying

CHAPTER NINETEEN: LORENE F. BARDY

Sometimes psychic detecting can provide clues that are right-on-target, yet the desired results of the investigation are not immediately achieved. The Steven Ivens chapter noted that the psychics had precise GPS coordinates for the location of Steven's body, yet a sinking sun and an inaccurate map service prevented Find Me and AZSTAR searchers to reach that location.

The case of Lorene Bardy proves that point.

Lorene went missing from her residence in Carnation, WA on April 26, 2012. She had a life-threatening health issue which required medication, so there was an immediate need to locate the missing 53 year old woman. The King County Sheriff's Office listed her as a missing and possibly endangered person.

Lorene's family contacted AZSTAR May 12th. The assignment to Find Me went out the same day.

Many of the psychics reported that she was deceased and could be found near her residence. Four members provided specific GPS coordinates in a small area near Lorene's home. Based on this information, AZSTAR conducted an intense search of the wooded area near the home, but was not able to locate the missing woman.

A month later two hikers on the main trail through King County Park on May 24 discovered human remains, which were soon identified as those of Lorene Bardy. Although, no foul play was indicated or suspected, the cause of death was listed as "pending" until the medical examiner issued a ruling.

The Find Me psychics had provided hits in the area where her body was found. Dwayne Brock, Sunny Dawn Johnston and Tammy Carpenter provided the closest hits. Brock's location was less than 500 ft. from where her body was eventually found.

The "close, but no cigar" part of this brief story is that Kristi Smith, AZSTAR Search Commander, was at one time searching that area. She said that if her team had been able to search longer they would have found Lorene three weeks earlier.

Confucius said, "The superior man makes the difficulty to be overcome his first interest; success comes only later." So, what has the group learned from such "close, but no cigar" searches? Much, it would seem. For one, the psychics have again proven not only the value of psychic research, but also the value of the Find Me approach to finding missing persons and solving crimes. Such incidents prove the value of working with equally talented and dedicated partners, such as AZSTAR – that such widely different teams can work well together and augment each other's efforts.

"...that one may smile and smile and be a villain..."

~Hamlet (William Shakespeare)

CHAPTER TWENTY: COLLEGE AGE VICTIMS

A disturbing pattern began emerging in 1984. With more than 100 psychics working any given case, the locations cited for the missing person will be all over the board. Again, no psychic is 100 percent accurate 100 percent of the time. When Baldwin or Brock are having bad days, Carpenter and Johnson will be having good days and vice versa. Sighting clusters are significant. If a large number of psychics hit on or around a specific area, chances are good that they've hit on a valid location. Narrowing a search area is of incredible value to law enforcement and search and rescue operations.

About the time Find Me began working on the Josh Szostak case, clusters of another type began showing up – clusters of multiple victims. These were primarily in the Midwest and Wisconsin, Minnesota and Illinois, but other clusters appearing in Iowa, Michigan, Indiana and Ohio. New York, New Jersey and the East Coast also had unusual clusters of victims. The number of victims was so large that Find Me had to develop a spreadsheet to keep track.

Here is a sampling of the cases presented to Find Me.

Chris Jenkins, wearing Indian Halloween costume was abducted in a van, held, tortured and drowned. He was found with his arms crossed across his chest, still wearing the costume.

Patrick Kycia, a well-liked, well-adjusted 19-year old college student with a 3.65 grade point average, made what was supposed to be a quick stop at a Phi Sigma Kappa fraternity house party, but ended up doing shots of whiskey with his friends. Sometime after midnight,

Kycia left the party for home but never made it. His body was found in the Red River four days later.

After a night of drinking, Jared Dion was seen getting on a bus headed back to campus. He was reliable, dependable, and a good student on target to graduate. Five days later his body was found in the Mississippi River by divers.

Eighteen-year old Dan Zamien, a freshman at the University of St. Thomas, left a party hosted by classmates near the St. Thomas campus. He was talking to a friend on his cell phone when the friend heard what she believed to be, "Oh my God. Help!" before the call ended abruptly.

On September 30, 2006, University of La Crosse junior Luke Homan celebrated with friends at the annual Oktoberfest in downtown La Crosse. He was last seen at approximately 2:15 a.m. at The Vibe bar. His body was found in ten feet of water near a levee in the Mississippi River.

Joshua Kaneakua, 19, was last seen on 3/1/07, St. Patrick's Day heaving Gabby's Saloon and Eatery in northeast Minneapolis. His body was discovered in the Mississippi River on 3/2707.

After drinking at a campus residence hall, 20-year old Adam Falcon headed to the Tick Tock Inn tavern in in Canton, NY, with his friends where he drank using a borrowed ID.

He was last seen leaving the tavern on Sunday, November 13th at 1:30 a.m.

Brian Welzien – his body found in Lake Michigan two months after disappearing.

Glen Ladley – his body found along the shore of Lake Michigan.

Jay Polhill – found in the Calumet River.

Ken Chrisiansen – drowned.

Nathan Kapfer – drowned.

Lucas Homan – drowned.

Bryan Barker – drowned.

Joshua Snell – drowned.

Kenji Ohmi – drowned.

The number of victims is staggering. As this book is being written, the count is **290** victims in this class.

What makes these disappearances a cluster instead of just a bunch of random missing persons?

Snyder says, "One of the important things to recognize from the spreadsheet and the photographs we have accumulated for all of the victims is that 97 percent of the victims are Caucasian males. There are no females and most important there are only two or three black males and only one or two oriental men. I believe this to be incredibly significant." Find Me is employing comparison analysis software through a data analysis data linking system and is confident of the findings. These are not random, unconnected acts of violence or accidental deaths of foolish young, white college-age men. The group has and continues to bring these cases to the attention of the FBI Behavior Science Unit because the BSU or the FBI is the only agency that can handle this type of broad spectrum investigation. The DEA could get involved, but needed to prove that a drug was introduced so that it would fall under the guidelines of accepting an investigation. The multiple jurisdictional nightmares created by attaching all of the cases in to one court or jurisdiction for prosecution would overwhelm any local or even a statewide law enforcement authority.

Snyder says, "In almost every single case it's the perfect crime for the simple reason that the water dissipates any and all evidence after the body has been in the water for a period of time. More specifically, any evidence that has any relation to a substance being put in the body – either put into the drink or injected into the body dissipates within a period of seven to twelve days." Advanced toxicology could potentially identify illegal substances, but most if not 95 percent of all medical examiners NEVER consider doing an advanced toxicology. If a body of a college student is found in water this practice should be mandatory.

Tests for debilitating drugs, such as GHB, are rarely considered. There's nothing sinister in that. To most investigators the cause of death is obvious: some kid got drunk, fell into the river and drowned. End of story. Except that Find Me believes there is a lot more to the story in many of these types of cases. The difference is perspective and jurisdiction and to an extent that's understandable. The police or sheriff sees one case of drowning due to intoxication. File the report and move on to the next crime. He never hears about the very similar case that happens several counties away or nearby, but in a different state. Find Me sees a broad pattern crossing numerous jurisdictions.

A Pattern of Disappearance and Murder

From the psychic perspective it's not a matter of a single killing here and a single killing there. Rather it's a dark pattern indicating a serial killer at work – probably a number of serial killers.

Here's the pattern. A young man, generally sophomore or junior in college age and almost universally white, goes out for a night of drinking with friends. He is generally athletic, personable and well-liked. He gets drunk or appears drunk and for any number of reasons leaves his friends, often wandering off on his own. He disappears or his body later turns up in a nearby river with the cause of death attributed to drowning due to intoxication.

Because of the significant amount of psychic research conducted into these cases on a multi-state project, Find Me urges law enforcement to conduct extensive testing of the bodies found in these types of cases. The only way to find a substance that has been injected into the body or introduced into the body is by doing a procedure of retrieving fluids from behind the eye of the victim and/or out of the lymph nodes of the victim because a drug induced into a body will stay behind the eye in the fluid and will stay in the lymph nodes for up to four months. If the body is found a week to ten days or even months after the body disappears then there is still a possibility through advanced toxicology analysis to find out if a drug, such as GHB, was induced into the victim. As this book is being written Find Me is looking into cases in 28 states. The group has found several similar circumstances in the State of Washington and several in the lower southern states and on the east coast and is trying to compare its results with those states to determine if bodies being recovered belong to the same killer or killers. The spreadsheet accumulates information as to where the person went missing and any facts relating to highways and other information. The group is making comparisons to see if a motive and/or similarities that will lead into a direction that we can solve the investigation.

Find Me psychics have identified currently 35 potential suspects in the college age killings case. These suspects are grouped into five factions. (For obvious reasons, until the cases are resolved, there a limitations on what can be written here.) One faction has a total of 16 suspects. One is a group of four people. Two people are apparently operating independently and another group of individuals could contain as many as 30 suspects. There is no connection between any of these groups that can be determined at this time. The only exception is a common taste for murder.

These murders appear to be happening within specific areas (comfort zones) of the various factions. One faction, involving sixteen or more people, is a traveling group of musicians or some of their groupies. This band**(s)** is well-known and is recognized for its music which often features lyrics about murder, torture and violent death. In these cases where the band is performing a concert in any particular city, we have found that a person goes missing the day before, the day of or the day after the concert. The disappearances occur usually in or near a state or city college where the group performs. The fact that this happens consistently tends to prove that groups going around with these bands are most likely involved in these missing kids.

Find Me has compiled a massive amount of detailed and specific information and is urging local law enforcement to look beyond their jurisdictions for connections to these apparent drowning's. They are not suicides. They are not accidental deaths. These kids are being set up and murdered in the vast majority. These young men are victims of well-planned, carefully-coordinated, and meticulously-executed serial killings.

Law enforcement – Look beyond your borders and see the big picture.

"...an organization is not merely a collection of individuals, but is a super-individual with like qualities, only larger. It should be as much more powerful spiritually than a single individual, as it is more powerful than a single individual."

~Alva Konkle

Chapter Twenty-one: Forming Your Own Psychic Group

This chapter isn't a how-to so much as it is a series of insights into founding a psychic detecting group. As with any organization, the group must adapt to applicable personnel, resources, needs and drives. Nonetheless, the information found here should be invaluable for those wanting to form a group of psychic sleuths.

"Psychic detecting and the use of psychic abilities is not an exact science. As a matter of fact, I don't think it's in the realm of science," Snyder says. That's an interesting statement from a man who founded an internationally recognized team of psychics. In a sense, he expressed a feeling that is one of the group's largest challenges from law enforcement today. "Well, all our leads are played out. Let's call those psychics; what have we got to lose?" The truth is, that by waiting the authorities, family and friends have a lot to lose.

Take the Leap

If you are interested in forming a group of psychic detectives, expect challenges and the need for taking leaps of faith. If you handle things correctly, you can also expect incredible personal rewards. Baldwin has often said, "Being a member of Find Me has been among the toughest, most frustrating, heart-breaking and yet most rewarding experiences of my life."

Those rewards are of a personal, mental, emotional and spiritual nature. One of the founding tenants of Find Me is that the group would never accept reward money from families or law enforcement. The second tenant states that no one can use the organization for personal glory. If financing the group is a main concern, as it is with many groups, you can seek tax exempt status so that you can accept donations. Snyder says, "The main focus of any group like ours is that everyone has to be doing this for reasons that are pure, and not with the thought of charging for services or reaping any form of financial benefit for our efforts."

It is recommend that you adopt these tenants from the beginning of your group and make them well-known to all who want to participate. One, think they are essential to the long-term success of a psychic group. Two, you will quickly learn who is joining for personal gain and who is interested in pursuing higher goals. Baldwin says, "Those who show up at the early meetings who are there for personal gain, will soon drop away. Since ancient times, men have known the wisdom of separating the wheat from the chaff."

ADOPT THE TEAM APPROACH

Unlike some television programs and motion pictures, psychics rarely get the full picture when practicing their skills. As in the Darrin Palmer case, one psychic will get an extremely detailed view of the scene, but have no idea where that scene might be. Another psychic will get a number, an impression, a smell or an image. Individually, each may be accurate, but without context virtually meaningless. Put all these clues together and you get a good bit of that full picture – often enough to solve the crime or find the missing person. This is the way the universe works and those are the rules. The teamwork approach lets the psychics work with and benefit from those rules rather than be confused or obstructed by them.

Set Criteria for Membership

It's your group. It's your call, but you will benefit from following the time-tested approaches of successful psychic organizations and then adapting methods and processes that fit your specific needs and challenges.

Your group should set up a vetting process, which should include interviewing prospective members about their abilities and success level. They should be willing to provide complete biographical and contact information. Each new member should agree to the rules and guidelines of the organization.

It's a good idea to adopt an official Code of Ethics.

It's also a good idea to put new members on probation. The length of time should be determined by your group's culture and needs. New members should, however, have all rights, privileges and responsibilities of full membership during this time. A probationary time is helpful for the team to evaluate the new member and for the new member to evaluate his or her commitment to the organization.

Develop a Process for Accepting Cases

Don't try to wing it or trust to your psychic abilities to run an organization. That word "organization" is key. The process should be simple, easy and effective. It will usually begin with a call or e-mail from a friend, a family member, someone in law enforcement or search and rescue. When you set up a website, be sure to offer a way to get in touch. The information can then be funneled to a coordinator who distributes it to the entire group using e-mail. Those who can work on the case do so and then file reports. All members should be required to file a report within the stated deadline in the e-mail.

Members who get nothing or who for whatever reason cannot work on a specific case should still send an email saying so. Reports should be collated into a single, cohesive document which and sent to the appropriate authority in the case. Phone calls between the coordinator and the officials in charge of the case at hand are common. With few exceptions, he or she should remain in contact with the authority throughout the investigation.

All reports should be sent to the authorities through a single channel. It is recommended that even when responding directly with a request from a family, you would be well-advised to work directly and only with the authority on the case. Contact with the family can be maintained, of course, but they should not be allowed "in the loop" on the investigation. To do so would create enormous nightmare scenarios and possibly create situations which could interfere with or even compromise the investigation. Withholding investigatory information from a worried or grieving family is challenging, especially when one or more of them are weeping in front of you. But for the sake of the investigation, they should not be given information until the case is closed or the authorities say it's okay.

Individual members shouldn't discuss the case at hand among themselves until after their reports are filed to prevent accidentally affecting each other's readings.

Stay Focused and Keep Organizing

If you're the organizer of your group, don't get discouraged. The response from your members will range from immediate and enthusiastic to practically non-existent. Some people will join for the highest motives. Others will hop onboard for a hoped-for free ride to fame and reward. Weeding the wheat from the chaff can be an unpleasant task, but it is a necessary part of the vetting process.

You will encounter skeptical authorities, and it's possible you'll occasionally face outright hostility. It's important to remember the reason you formed the group in the first place. The good you will accomplish will far outweigh the hassles you face along the way.

Expect to evolve

Expect evolution when forming and maintaining a psychic-detecting group. That's okay; it's a normal part of the process. Every group experiences growing pains.

Partnering With a Search and Rescue Team

The Find Me sister organization, Arizona Search Track and Rescue or AZ-STAR, is one of the finest, most professional and best trained groups in the nation. The partnership is a long and successful one and one that is mutually beneficial. Of course, those who benefit most are the friends and families of lost persons or victims of crimes and the law enforcement agencies who use our information to catch criminals and close cases.

The Dylan Redwine case is an example of how this teamwork pays off. The initial search area for the missing boy could be described as all of southern Colorado or at least the counties near Durango – an enormous and mountainous area covered with dense forest. Find Me psychics not only reduced that search area down to a single mountain, but to specific GPS points on that mountain. By combining talents, the two organizations did what no other group was able to do – locate Dylan's remains, providing invaluable support to the LaPlata County Sheriff's Office in that case.

Wherever you are, it is likely that there is a search and rescue team in your state – probably several of them. Search and rescue is far more complex than just having a bunch of people wandering through forest and field. Efforts could involve "ground pounding" grid searches through all kinds of terrain. For example, in Arizona rescue teams can be called on to trek through conditions ranging from blistering deserts to snow and ice covered mountains or from lakes and rivers to underground caves and abandoned mines. Intense training is essential. That goes for the scent, track and cadaver dogs.

The best search and rescue groups are those that are the best trained and those that have the best reputation. Good intentions and sound motives are not enough. If you want to partner with a search and rescue group – do homework. Check out the website of any group you are considering. Speak with the local authorities and research their reputation. Which are the most professional and most reliable groups in your area? The most critical qualifications for search and rescue (SAR) teams are training and certification.

Certification is available from a number of sources, but real certification can come only from qualified instructors. Some groups will say that their animals are certified, but *how* they are certified is critical. They must meet the most stringent standards.

Evidence procedure and protection of the crime scene is extremely important because your efforts could enhance or hinder a crime-scene investigation. Often, a search scene can turn into a crime scene when it becomes clear that an abduction or murder has taken place. Be constantly aware of your responsibility to enhance, rather than hinder, the search process.

It is imperative that any psychic wishing to volunteer with a search and rescue team know what he (or she) is setting himself up for. Grid searches are grueling and can be dangerous to life and limb. Several times in various searches a slip or a stumble has nearly led to a potentially deadly fall off a rock face or a cliff. During warm seasons search and rescue personnel wear snake leggings for good reason. By their nature psychics aren't generally geared for grid search mentality. They go with the flow of intuition. A psychic on a search must be willing to follow the rules and the directions of the search commander. The SAR team shouldn't be pulled out of one search to spend time looking for a wandering psychic.

There's another consideration. Sometimes search and rescue becomes search and recovery. This is especially true when psychics are called in as a last resort. A perfect illustration is the Ed Hatfield case. When the Find Me/AZ-STAR teams found Ed's remains, they had to stay with the decomposed body. They had to mark off the area as a crime scene and wait several hours until they could turn over the scene to the proper authorities. You can imagine what those hours were like for the teams on site. Psychics volunteering for search and rescue should give careful consideration to their own mental and emotional responses to dealing with highly unpleasant situations.

DEVELOP SOLID RELATIONSHIPS WITH LEGAL AUTHORITIES

Recognize your place in the bureaucratic food chain. No matter how many psychics work a case and regardless of the hard work and dedication of those psychics, your group is not the lead investigator on the case. Finding the missing person, the body, the get-away vehicle or the desired evidence is just the beginning of a long process. Evidence must be collected and processed according to strict legal guidelines. You just don't have the training or the authority to process a crime scene – so don't. It's essential that you understand how the legal agencies you will be dealing with work, so can augment, rather than hamper, their work.

Most people go to work with the best intentions in mind and this applies to the police and other legal authorities. How well they carry out their duties depends on a number of factors: personal experience, individual commitment, size of the force, amount of training, street knowledge, gut instinct, specialty training, financial and other resources, and case load. Each factor can have a dramatic effect on any given case. That's especially true when you throw in a bunch of psychics. Most police departments pair an experienced senior officer with a junior officer so that the rookie can benefit from the knowledge and experience of the older and (hopefully) wiser officer. You could end up working with either one or both types.

Some departments overload their officers, which creates a backlog and a lot of time passes without much really being accomplished. Waiting on evidence from a forensic lab usually adds a significant amount of time to the investigation, often six to twelve weeks or so on lab reports and processing. The officers assigned to the case may be just as dedicated as you are to solve the case, but they may be hamstrung by factors outside their control. Psychics shouldn't add to that burden; they should relieve it.

You'll periodically encounter exceptions to the dedicated cop. Some professional investigators drag their feet, some are incompetent, and others won't hesitate to lie to you. Even though you and your team are volunteers, it's important to adopt a professional attitude. Look at every situation and act according to the long-term view of solving the case. Despite the shortcomings of any given officer or investigator, you'll want to maintain a strong relationship with the department.

Think in terms of achieving the greatest good over the longest period of time. The fact is, if they're listening to you and accepting your information, you're well ahead of the game. Even those who do not believe in psychic phenomena can be willing to support your efforts. Baldwin relates a conversation he had with a deputy sheriff while on a search in rural Arizona. The deputy said, "I don't believe in this psychic business, but your guys' information matches our information, stuff we haven't released to the public, so well that I'm out here searching with you."

Have Someone Who Can "Talk Cop" to the Cops

Having someone who can "talk cop" to the authorities is an invaluable aid in working with the authorities. Authorities are willing to do whatever they can to help families, but are sometimes unable or unwilling to work with psychics because of their lack of knowledge about the issue. Having someone in law enforcement as a buffer to the police on behalf of the family is the best way to go in these matters, especially when dealing with psychics.

The police will accept and investigate information from an anonymous phone call. Psychic information should at least be given that much credibility.

Another reason some authorities are reluctant to accept information from psychics is that they often get so many calls from psychics, along with witnesses, concerned citizens and others. Large departments can handle most of the telephone traffic, but small departments get frustrated with the calls, especially if they have little or no knowledge about psychics.

Individual psychics who contact the police often get a less than positive response and this is a real challenge. It can become easy to just give up. "The world needs more groups like Find Me, so that more and more police departments can use this extremely powerful tool," Snyder says. Working with vetted psychics working as a professional group is the only way to go, since most of the individual psychics calling police departments are lacking skills and frustrate the police with hundreds of different scenarios.

You Are Not the Cops

Let the police do the policing.

Psychics who receive information about a case that's nearby have a natural desire to get into the field and conduct some hands-on investigating. Many times, they'll do so without permission from, or even contact with, the investigating authority.

That attitude is misguided, foolish and dangerous. First, you are potentially putting yourself in harm's way. To put it bluntly, you could get yourself killed. Some of the people or groups you will be investigating are dangerous, and some will be killers. Find Me and AZ-STAR have conducted searches within "spitting distance" of the homes of suspected murderers. A killer might think twice about causing trouble with a group of people (witnesses), large and well-trained dogs, and searchers who are armed with semiautomatic pistols. That same killer might not be so intimidated about a single person or a small group snooping around his home or property.

A second consideration is the danger of contaminating a crime scene.

Examining a crime scene and processing the evidence is the sole responsibility of the investigating authority. Psychic investigators should protect the scene and not leave the area until the proper investigative officers arrives. Again, your responsibility is to protect the scene, not investigate it. Your good intentions may cause more problems than you foresee.

Two benefits develop from this approach. One, by preserving the crime scene you strengthen the case against the perpetrator. Two, by following the rules you will gain the respect of law enforcement. Don't underestimate the value of a good reputation. Word travels fast and negative PR can damage your efforts for years. Conversely, by showing professionalism, your willingness to follow the rules will gain friends, earn respect and open doors to greater opportunities to serve.

You can probably find a great source of advice by contacting a retired police officer, a federal or state agent, or even a private detective who shows an interest in your work. The prosecutor's office in the jurisdiction of the case you're investigating might welcome your information. The officer might not be interested at all, but, if you are confident that the information you're getting is on target, don't give up on the authorities. Be professional and be persistent and your efforts will pay off.

Most departments have a public information officer to handle incoming information when detectives are covered up. You can certainly try that area.

As a last resort, you can approach the command staff. That would include the chief, assistant chief, commander, captain, lieutenant and sergeant. Remember, although they are public servants, these are very busy people, facing a lot of challenges. Always maintain a professional attitude and show proper respect.

Help Groups

Another quick search of the Internet will reveal a large number of foundations, organizations and missing children/adults groups. It can be a real challenge to determine which are best suited to help you and your group the most. As of this date, these are some of the active organizations you should consider.

National Center for Missing and Exploited Children – www.ncmec.org

Child Seek Network – www.childseeknetwork.com

Child Watch of North America – www.childwatch.org

Child Protection Education of America – www.find-missing-children.org

Morgan Nick Foundation – www.morgannick.com

"Minds are like parachutes.
They only function when they are open."
~Sir James Dewar

Chapter Twenty Two: A Call to Law Enforcement Agencies: Treat Vetted Psychics as First Responders

Law enforcement and related agencies should consider groups with vetted psychics a first responder when someone goes missing or when a crime is committed. It doesn't make sense to ignore a valuable and proven resource until all other avenues have been exhausted. The hesitation some law enforcement personnel have about working with psychics is understandable, but not rational. It's easy to determine whether or not a psychic group is a bunch of ambulance chasers or a dedicated group of investigators. Just ask about their policies, procedures and codes of conduct. Serious groups will be happy to discuss how they can best work with your organization.

Psychic detecting works. As former law enforcement officer and private investigator Steven C. Kopp wrote, "During my thirty-five years of work in both the public and private sectors, I have made use of psychic resources on hundreds of investigations. Overall, my success in locating missing individuals has improved dramatically since first using a psychic resource in 1985."

The authorities readily accept and act upon anonymous information, such as a phone call or an email. Certainly information provided by a team of experts in their fields working directly on a specific case should be given the same consideration – at least!

The people in a professional psychic group know to work exclusively through the appropriate legal authority even when they've been called in by families. They will know to provide information to your organization and not to divulge important information about an ongoing case to family and friends. They'll also know the importance of confidentiality and managing information when approached by the news media. Provide a single contact who can "talk cop" to work with the authorities handling the case. The goal is to solve the crime, find the missing person, and help bring the guilty to justice. Do not doesn't interfere with an investigation; augment and enhance it. Law enforcement agencies should consider people with psychic gifts as tools of the trade. People with these gifts should be allowed and encouraged to use them. That is especially true when those people have organized themselves into an effective team. You should welcome help and insight from all reliable sources.

Talented and vetted psychics are reliable sources. If you share one of the following beliefs, reconsider your opinion.

"We don't believe in psychics."

"We have never heard of a case being solved by psychics."

"We are concerned about public opinion."

"We just don't want to go there."

Dedicated psychics want to change those attitudes. If you've never used a psychic, or met a psychic, or researched cases that psychics have worked on and solved, then how can you make those assessments? It makes zero sense to take a position like that without knowing anything about the process.

If you're approached by a psychic group, give them a trial run. You have nothing to lose. If they come up with nothing, you're no worse off. If they provide valuable information, however, you are significantly closer to solving your case. Again, even if you are a skeptic, you have nothing to lose and everything to gain. Don't let ignorance, ego or lack of knowledge keep you from accepting potentially valuable information.

More law enforcement agencies are willing to work with psychics than ever. While working with a retired New York City detective on a missing-person case in Florida, Snyder was told, "I'll take information from the devil if I can find a missing child." During another missing-person investigation, in Arizona, an FBI agent stated, "I have never solved an investigation on my own and can always use some help." An Arizona police detective told Baldwin, "Off the record, my biggest case last year was solved by a psychic."

If you're considering working with psychics, you're not as alone as you may think. Doors and minds are opening. More and more people and organizations are seeking out psychic detectives and finding them a valuable resource in finding missing persons and solving crimes.

Most psychics aren't asking you to believe in this type of phenomenon. They're not in the missionary business. They just want to provide information to help you with your cases. Accept the gift for what it is. Accept the information and see if it parallels facts that you're already aware of in your investigation. Secondly, if your investigation is going nowhere, then look at the psychic information as potential new leads or clues that may help solve your investigation.

Provide feedback so that the psychics can continue to hone our skills and improve our work. If there is a single, overriding complaint expressed by psychic detectives and members of psychic groups, it's the lack of feedback. They understand the legal reasons for withholding some information during an ongoing investigation, but at some point that information can be shared. It should be shared so they will know where they were on target and where they were not. That kind of information is invaluable in helping the psychics evaluate and improve their skills. It also helps the group to improve its processes and methods of working with the authorities

Don’t sit on potentially valuable information, regardless of the reception you think you might receive. Lives could be at stake.

About the Author

Dan Baldwin is an inaugural member of FIND ME, a volunteer group of psychics, retired and active law enforcement personnel, legal and investigative experts, and search and rescue teams committed to finding missing persons and solving crimes. He served as a member of the Board of Directors and as that board's President. He also participated as a "ground pounder" in searches with AZ-STAR. He is the author, co-author or ghostwriter of more than 50 books on business. He is the author of the Caldera series of westerns, *Trapp Canyon* and *Bock's Canyon* Western novels, the mysteries *Desecration, Heresy* and *Vengeance*, the thriller *Sparky and the King*, the non-fiction works *The Practical Pendulum*, the as-told-to-book *Find Me,* and *Just the Facts, Please, About Alcohol and Drug Abuse* (with George Sewell). He is the winner of numerous local, regional, and national awards for writing and directing film and video projects. He earned an Honorable Mention from the Society of Southwestern Authors writing competition for his short story *Flat Busted* and earned a Finalist designation from the National Indie Excellence Awards for *Trapp Canyon* and for *Caldera III – A Man of Blood,* and a Finalist designation for *Sparky and the King* in the 2015 New Mexico-Arizona Book Awards competition. Baldwin is a resident of Phoenix-Mesa, Arizona.

PRAISE FOR *THE PRACTICAL PENDULUM – GETTING INTO THE SWING OF THINGS*

by Dan Baldwin

The Practical Pendulum is a no-nonsense guidebook to pendulum dowsing designed to teach the novice and enhance the skills of the experienced practitioner. Baldwin is an experienced dowser who uses his skills to help find missing persons and to solve crimes. His approach is to demonstrate how to effectively use an incredible-yet-practical tool, an instrument that bridges the gap between a higher power and the human subconscious. The information you want to know is knowable – everything from where you lost your car keys to addressing everyday challenges and opportunities to discovering the purpose of life. The pendulum provides a proven way of accessing that information directly and through your own efforts. Topics covered include defining the pendulum and pendulum dowsing, selecting a pendulum, dangers to avoid and benefits to seek, pendulum language, problem solving tips, diagnosing problems, map dowsing, and a step-by-step how-to guide to conducting a successful pendulum session. Baldwin says a pendulum is nothing more than a weight on a string – a tool – but it is a practical tool that can open to new levels of self-awareness, personal achievement and a happier and more successful life.

* * *

"THE PRACTICAL PENDULUM is exactly that… practical. This fabulous book makes even a novice comfortable, skilled and respectful of the way of the pendulum. However, it isn't just for the novice.

As a psychic medium with 30+ years of experience in metaphysics, I learned a few things too. I highly recommend that anyone, new or skilled, read this book!"

~Sunny Dawn Johnson
Spiritual Teacher and Author
The Sunlight Alliance

"Dan has been with Find Me since its inception in 2001 and his pendulum abilities have surfaced on numerous occasions and were strikingly accurate in locating missing persons. Dan's abilities and knowledge of the pendulum can only enhance anyone's abilities that puts in an effort. A must read for anyone interested in the pendulum."

~J.E. "Kelly" Snyder
CEO/Founder Find Me Group

"I love the book – a very practical guide book. "The Practical Pendulum is a must to have in your library on dowsing. It's straight forward and very easy to understand and learn. A Must for both beginners and even advanced practitioners will enjoy this book. It is also a great teaching tool for teachers."

~Dave Campbell,
Psychic and Medium

"I have known Dan through our connection of The Find Me group over a ten year period. We have been able to share many experiences through our Psychic work together, for which I am truly grateful.
"He shares his many Gift's and teaching's in this book about how to use a pendulum, a book I fully endorse. This is a book you will want to have. I am so pleased to have him as my friend and colleague."

~Jeanette Healey,
Psychic Detective

"Of all the self-help books I've read regarding tools used to enhance your own abilities, Dan's is by far the best! Easy to understand and it creates a sense of urgency and excitement to develop your own pendulum dowsing skills. I would recommend this book to all! You'll be amazed at the results!"

~Rhonda Hull,
Psychic Investigator

The Practical Pendulum is available in e-book and paperback formats from Amazon, CreateSpace, Barnes & Noble, Smashwords and other major distributors.

* * *

ALSO BY DAN BALDWIN

Find Me (As Told to Dan Baldwin)
Just the Facts, Please, About Alcohol and Drug Abuse (With George Sewell)
Streetwise Landlording and Property Management (With Mark B. Weiss)
Streetwise Restaurant Management (With John R. James)
Caldera
Caldera II – A Man on Fire
Caldera III – A Man of Blood
Desecration – An Ashley Hayes Mystery
Heresy – An Ashley Hayes Mystery
Vengeance – An Ashely Hayes Mystery
Trapp Canyon
Bock's Canyon
Sparky and the King
Vampire Bimbos on Spring Break (Short Story Collection)

Made in the USA
Charleston, SC
09 January 2016